ENDORSEMENTS

In *Miraculous Identity*, Linda Breitman demystifies what it means to connect with God, to have a relationship with our Creator. Christians are often confounded by these concepts but are embarrassed to ask, "What does it really mean and how do I get there?" I am grateful that Linda has shown us how to cross the threshold of our human existence and enter the heavenly realms. Once you've experienced this kind of intimacy with God, you will want to keep coming back. Those moments with God have been life-changers for me.
Michele Rigby Assad, Former CIA Intelligence Officer and author of *Breaking Cover: My Secret Life in the CIA and What it Taught Me About What's Worth Fighting For*

This refreshing, timely book by Linda Breitman covers the full spectrum of our Christian life. It's not an ordinary book. It contains the matchless keys to become all God created you to be – to fulfill your destiny. As you integrate the principles taught into your daily life, you will walk in a new dimension of the Holy Spirit. I highly recommend *Miraculous Identity* as an invaluable source of encouragement to you.
Gary Oates, Author of *Open My Eyes, Lord*

Our salvation is miraculous! Kingdom is living beyond salvation and into the supernatural life of our new man and true Identity. Linda Breitman's book, *Miraculous Identity*, is an invitation to come into a deeper revelation of intimacy with the God. Linda mentors the reader as she cleverly presents principals and insights, with prayers and activations, any believer can grasp and appropriate into their lives. This is a must read for those hungering to live in His presence!
Maria Sainz, Red Seal Ministries, San Diego, CA

The framework used by Linda for this identity study series is simplicity at its best. No matter where you are in your Christian walk *Miraculous Identity* is for you. From personal study, small group study, all the way to a conference style with interactive events, this book will bring freedom. The still small voice of Holy Spirit will touch you through Linda's words and engaging the proclamations found within its pages will shatter unseen strongholds in your life.
Pastor Mike Ferry, Cornerstone Christian Fellowship, Redmond, OR, author of "*Making Disciples, Releasing into Ministry*"

I love Linda's approach in *Miraculous Identity*. We have been friends for years, and I have seen her walk out the very things she is teaching here. She meets things head on, lays it out in a direct, clear, and concise manner, and then positions you into activations that are so direct and compelling! There is no intimidation—anyone can go where she's gone. She helps you remove every barrier, every hindrance and all excuses. There is no reason not to progress in more of God. We have used Linda's first book *The Real You - Believing Your True Identity'* in a study group at our church –and literally, lives were changed. Thank you, Linda, for your hard work and yielding to God's adventure in your life. It was for us.
Pastor Judy Ross, Cloud 9 Worship Center, San Diego, CA

Miraculous Identity takes the reader on a beautiful "river cruise" right into a 3D surround sound experience with the Trinity. Scripture commands us to "Come boldly to the throne of grace that we may find grace to help in time of need;" the exhortations and rich scriptural meditations provided in this book escorts one to the throne and increases understanding that we are destined to LIVE there! This heaven-bound journey delights the soul and will accelerate miraculous transformation in every passenger.
Pastor Claudia Porter, Torch Life Church, Denver, CO

Not only does this book encourage and teach us all to go deeper with God, Linda Breitman understands that words are creative. Her scripture declarations are prophetic "smart bombs" that renew our minds, strengthen our faith, and heal our damaged emotions. Great job!

Pastor Juanita Childress, Jubilee Legacy International, Jubilee Christian Center, San Jose, California

Perfect for prison ministries, Bible studies and ministry schools! I have used Linda's identity teachings in my jail and prison ministry and the results are phenomenal! *Miraculous Identity* takes us even deeper in experiencing God more intimately!

Pastor Pat Winn,
Redeemed Ones Jail and Prison Ministry, Inc. Aurora, CO

Linda is one of those wonderful gifts that God has given to the body of Christ that not only teaches believers who they are in Christ, she is also a personal revelation herself of this truth. As you read this book, you will feel the freedom pouring over you, releasing the chains of condemnation from over your life.

Dr. Robert Cathers, Jr, Pastor, The Gathering Place, Simi, CA

Miraculous Identity causes vision, hope and intention to rise up within the reader, including me! Even though I know I have been transformed by these beautiful words of life over the forty-two years of extravagant pursuit of my Bridegroom King, I found myself strengthened and encouraged again as I read. The scripture says, "A well-spoken word at just the right time is like golden apples in settings of silver". This is one of those books written in the right season when God 's people must know who they are in HIM and who He is in them.

Linda does a superb job in imparting His identity very simply but powerfully that will miraculously change anyone who will believe and take the time to be diligent in establishing these revelatory truths into their foundation.

Be blessed abundantly as you are renewed, reformed and reidentified as 'one who belongs to the King'.

Billie Alexander, Limitless Realms Int'l Ministries,
San Diego, CA

Miraculous Identity is inspirational! Have you experienced a "watershed moment" in your life—that moment in time when your life changed and you knew that it would not ever be the same again? Linda Breitman will open your heart, soul and mind to a greater intimacy with God. This book can literally change your life. For people of faith or who are lost—it is a "must read". It is poignant, compelling and teaches you how to make that spiritual connection with God. I loved it and so will you.

Blanquita Cullum,
Veteran Broadcast Journalist and Former Governor, United States Broadcasting Board of Governor

Miraculous Identity will radically shift your life! All who read this book will know who they are, whose they are, and the miracle of their spiritual DNA--all that is at their disposal as a chosen, cherished child of God! Full of Scripture and creatively interactive, you will experience security and joy even in life's hardest circumstances as you determine to live in the love and power of the Holy Spirit flowing naturally though you every day. Miraculous!

Nancy Stafford
Actress, Speaker, and Author of *The Wonder of His Love: A Journey into the Heart of God*

Miraculous Identity
Study Guide

Linda Breitman

Published by Linda Breitman Ministries.
© 2018 by Linda Breitman

ISBN-13: 978-0-9894113-8-7

Unless otherwise indicated

All Scripture quotations are from The Passion Translation®. Copyright © 2017, 2018 by Passion & Fire Ministries, Inc. Used by permission. All rights reserved. ThePassionTranslation.com.

Additional Scripture quotations are from:

Scriptures taken from the Holy Bible, New International Version®, NIV®. Copyright © 1973, 1978, 1984, 2011 by Biblica, Inc.™ Used by permission of Zondervan. All rights reserved worldwide. The "NIV" and "New International Version" are trademarks registered in the United States Patent and Trademark Office by Biblica, Inc.™

Scripture quotations marked (AMP) are taken from the Amplified Bible, Copyright © 1954, 1958, 1962, 1964, 1965, 1987 by The Lockman Foundation. Used by permission.

Scripture quotations taken from the New American Standard Bible˚, Copyright © 1960, 1962, 1963, 1968, 1971, 1972, 1973, 1975, 1977, 1995 by The Lockman Foundation Used by permission.

Scripture taken from the New King James Version®. Copyright © 1982 by Thomas Nelson, Inc. Used by permission. All rights reserved.

The Holy Bible, English Standard Version (ESV) is adapted from the Revised Standard Version of the Bible, copyright Division of Christian Education of the National Council of the Churches of Christ in the U.S.A. All rights reserved.

Printed in the United States of America

ALL RIGHTS RESERVED
No part of this publication may be reproduced, stored in a retrieval system, or transmitted, in any form or by any means – electronic, mechanical, photocopying, recording, or otherwise – without prior written permission.

For information contact:
Linda Breitman Ministries
LindaBreitman.com

I dedicate this book to my beloved husband, King Turkey! My grammar expert, wonderful advisor, and singer of my favorite song, "I love a duckie, quackie, quack, quack!"

He started living in heaven right after I started this book, yet his memory lives on in these pages.

Quack!

Contents

Laying the Foundation 9

CHAPTER 1   Intimacy with the Nature of God 19

CHAPTER 2   The Secret Place 33

CHAPTER 3   The Wind of the Spirit 45

CHAPTER 4   Humility 57

CHAPTER 5   Supernaturally Faithful 69

CHAPTER 6   Trusting God 79

CHAPTER 7   Miraculous Peace 91

CHAPTER 8   Wondrous Realms of Knowing and Experiencing God 103

CHAPTER 9   Getting Pictures from God 115

CHAPTER 10   Encourage Yourself in the Lord 127

About Linda 137

Resources 139

MINISTRY SCHOOLS, BIBLE STUDY GROUPS, AND INDIVIDUAL STUDY:

This is an eleven-week course. The first week you will receive your book and workbook and begin by reading and discussing *Laying the Foundation*. If you are in a group, read it out loud, together. At one point, you will be directed to watch and discuss the first video.

Laying the Foundation

*Eternal life means to **know** and **experience** you as the only true God, and to know and experience Jesus Christ, as the Son whom you have sent.*
John 17:3 Passion Translation.

Many, many times in life, you face a situation you cannot fix. Actually, no one can fix it. Not a counselor, a doctor, the government—no one. When you finally come to the end of yourself, you settle in on the irrevocable reality that God is all you've got. Only God. He knows everything and can do anything. You desire to get closer to Him, to talk to Him, to bury your face in the folds of His robe. Moving closer to God and finding intimacy with Him is the heart of your *Miraculous Identity*. You and your Creator meeting together in *the secret place* where you can know and experience Him.

God wired you to know Him personally and intimately—and to *experience* Him. He designed you to enjoy a deep, engaging relationship with Him. The problem is most of us do not know how to get close to Him. We assume He is so far away and so very unknowable. But He is not. Within you right now, a hidden journey is taking place. It is an unfolding journey of your *Miraculous Identity*.

What is my miraculous identity? you ask. Your true, miraculous identity encompasses many facets. One vital component is for you to see yourself as God sees you. It is for you to experience all He says about who you are, why he created you, realizing your life purpose, and experiencing everything God is for you. He designed you to be in relationship with Him and live your life in all the miraculous wonders He promised you.

This course meets you where you are right now in your *hidden journey*. Opening these pages is rather like floating down a river of living water—sometimes you drift slowly and other times you experience the exhilaration of rushing waters! Revelation of your personal, one-on-one relationship with God will become clearer. He knows you. And He knows how to engage with you.

HOW TO GO THROUGH MIRACULOUS IDENTITY

This ten-chapter book will give you a renewing-your-mind upgrade in your *Miraculous Identity*. In Christ, your miraculous identity already exists, you are simply coming into agreement with it. The course is interactive and proactive. Each chapter contains:

- Teaching Section
- Posturing Declarations
- Experiential Activations
- Prayer Focus
- Heavenly Word

TEACHING

Each teaching section will bring understanding to a facet of your identity and stir your emotions with an increased desire for deeper relationship with God. You are designed to feel God in your emotions. He gave you emotions so you could feel things. You are *supposed* to experience God with your emotions. The fruit of the Spirit is love, joy, peace, patience, kindness, goodness, faithfulness, gentleness, and self-control—all involving your emotions.

God designed you to not just know that He loves you but to *experience* His love. Yes! *Experience* His love in your relationship with Him! He created you to feel His love so much that your response is to believe Him and trust Him and desire Him. *You* are His beloved.

The Teaching Section prepares you for the Posturing Declarations.

POSTURING DECLARATIONS

The Posturing Declarations are personalized verses from the Old and New Testaments written in first person for you to speak twice a day for seven days. Each declaration strengthens the reality of your miraculous identity. You will take a proactive role to rewire your thinking about your true identity. Dismantling old thoughts is something only *you* can do. Each chapter will help you create a new habit of renewing your mind. When you renew your mind, a miraculous transformation takes place. *Your* part is to renew your mind; *God* does the transformation inside you. Romans 12:2 Passion Translation reads:

Stop imitating the ideals and opinions of the culture around you but be inwardly transformed by the Holy Spirit through a total reformation of how you think. This will empower you to discern God's will as you live a beautiful life, satisfying and perfect in his eyes.

Since you will speak the declarations twice a day for one week, I suggest you take one week for each chapter. You don't have to. This course is for you to absorb any way you want. It is not an opportunity to beat yourself up if you don't get everything done. I encourage you to speak the Posturing Declarations and take your time with the additional activations to glean the greatest benefit from this book. If you do nothing else, speak the declarations. Declarations are the heart of this course. Incredible transformation takes place if you *do* the course and not just *read* the course.

EXPERIENTIAL ACTIVATIONS

Activations are interactive and will involve all your senses. They will help you personally engage with a new aspect of identity. So, take your time and enjoy the process. Don't rush through it. Each activation section begins with a guide and tracking system for doing the Posturing Declarations. Continue over the week to do the rest of the activations.

I can promise this course will change your life to the extent that you slow down and *do the work.* If you just read through it, not much change will occur. This is *your* time. Immerse yourself in each chapter. Soak in each declaration. Meditate on the declarations. Take the time to allow the *process* to take place. This is not a *study*—it is *transforming*.

PRAYER FOCUS AND HEAVENLY WORD

The Prayer Focus is just a starting place for you, a launching pad. Add your own words. The Heavenly Word reflects God's view of your miraculous identity.

THE FULL COURSE

The full course can be used for Bible Study groups, ministry schools, entire church study, and individual study. It includes this book, a workbook, and a video set. The workbook asks questions about the teaching and gives you a place to do your work. The video set includes eleven videos complementing each chapter.

Three Premises

Knowing these three premises before you begin this journey will help you succeed in applying the course. Come back to them to remind yourself. Write them on post-its. Believe me, it will help you. Your transformation is not without opposition.

Premise #1

Be relentless in renewing your mind and building your true identity.

First of all, recognize the warfare. All the forces of hell want to prevent you from knowing of and believing in your miraculous identity. Tremendous war surrounds your identity. Think about it. During the forty days Jesus was in the wilderness, the devil came more than once to challenge His identity with, "If you are the Son of God…" And every time, Jesus responded with, "It is written…" Circumstances will arise to keep you from speaking the declarations. Your mind will even fight you on it. You may even think it's not working or it's a dumb thing to do or you don't have time. Time is an issue for all of us. You are the one in charge of your time. Steward your time well. Recognize the war around renewing your mind. It is a battle, but it is a battle you can win.

Premise #2

You can make biblical declarations of what God says is true for and about you before you see the manifestation in your life.

Sometimes people think they cannot say a biblical truth unless they completely believe it now or have had it already come to pass in their life. I have heard people say, "I can't say that. I don't believe it." This is exactly what renewing the mind achieves: dismantling lies and replacing them with the truth. All of the promises of God are true *now*. Your miraculous identity is inside you *now*. When you speak biblical promises, you are aligning your thoughts with heaven. Life and death are in the power of the tongue. Speak life.

Premise #3

Recognize Holy Spirit is guiding you and speaking to you as your inner journey unfolds. Talk with Him.

You are a creative being in partnership with the most enjoyable, creative One—the Holy Spirit. Talk with Him as you approach each chapter. Engage fully with Him. He is your Guide. He is your Counselor. He is your Revealer. He is your Friend. Trust Him to help you.

This course is not an opportunity to beat yourself up if you get behind or don't fill in every blank or answer every question. Miraculous Identity is a guide, an interactive tool for you to use. Time after time, I hear people who have gone through my prequel to this study, *The Real You—Believing Your True Identity*, say the identity course was life changing. Yes, do the work, but don't fall into performance or perfection. I speak grace over you.

WATCH THE FIRST VIDEO NOW

Write down thoughts, ideas, concepts as you watch the video. There is space for video notes as well as discussion notes at the end of this section.

Discussion Questions

1. What impacted you about the video?

2. What is your reaction to the two trees teaching?

3. Do you want to deeply explore your Miraculous Identity? The choice is yours. I strongly suggest you make an agreement with the others going through this transformation with you that you will commit to doing the work. If you are doing the course alone, make the commitment to yourself. Plan your schedule now. Plan now to posture twice a day. If you need to get up a bit earlier, commit yourself to it. Look at what you are giving your time to now. Most likely, you will have to say "no" to something to make room for that which is new. It is vital you create space for renewing your mind. Remember: *you* renew; God *transforms*. When is the best time to focus on the book and study guide? And, above all, speak the declarations daily so your mind can meditate on and be renewed by the personalized verses.

4. As you lean into your Miraculous Identity, living waters *within* you will be stirred, and *you* will be stirred to draw near to God and to desire Him. A place deep inside you will seek Him. Picture two electrical cords wanting to connect. It is a fitting together born out of how and why you were created. You were made to love and be loved. God knows you better than anyone and loves you more than anyone ever could.

   Consider the following references to the secret place. What do these verses tell you about the secret place? What does the secret place mean to you personally? How have you experienced this?

One thing I have desired of the LORD, that I will seek: that I may dwell in the house of the LORD all the days of my life, to behold the beauty of the LORD and to inquire in His temple. For in the day of trouble He will hide me in His shelter; In the secret place of His tent He will hide me; He will lift me up on a rock (Psalm 27:4-5 AMP).

He who dwells in the secret place of the Most High shall abide under the shadow of the Almighty. I will say of the LORD, "He is my refuge and my fortress; my God, in Him I will trust. (Psalm 91:1-2 NKJV).

5. Your thoughts advance or hinder your inner hidden journey. The Bible calls this renewing your mind. Read the following verse and answer these questions: How could a total reformation of the way you think take place? What happens to your inner, hidden journey when this reformation occurs?

Stop imitating the ideals and opinions of the culture around you but be inwardly transformed by the Holy Spirit through a total reformation of how you think. This will empower you to discern God's will as you live a beautiful life, satisfying and perfect in his eyes (Romans 12:2 Passion Translation).

According to the following verse, what do we do with our thoughts? What is the war? How do you think we fight it?

For though we live in the world, we do not wage war as the world does. The weapons we fight with are not the weapons of the world. On the contrary, they have divine power to demolish strongholds. We demolish arguments and every pretension that sets itself up against the knowledge of God, and we take captive every thought to make it obedient to Christ (2 Corinthians 10:3-5).

6. Read Ephesians 4:22-24 in a few different translations. What is the old self and how do we handle it? What do we do with our minds?

You are now ready to begin the hidden journey of your miraculous identity. I pray wondrous, wild, exhilarating encounters and revelations upon you. I pray fresh insights and closeness. I pray you experience God's love. And I pray much laughter.

Video Notes

Video Notes

1
Intimacy with the Nature of God

Just Be Real

God created us to draw near to Him, the way we would draw near to a good friend and get to know all about him or her. Having a very personal—even intimate—relationship with God is our inheritance. Jesus paid for it with His life. God is wooing you into a deeper, closer relationship with Him. You don't have to have everything all figured out. He knows how to reveal Himself to you in a way that you will know Him as your most loving, most reliable, most faithful friend. Take a deep breath and breathe in God's acceptance. Breathe in His desire for you. Now, relax and open your heart.

READ PARAGRAPHS 1 TO 9 IN CHAPTER ONE, AND ANSWER THE FOLLOWING QUESTIONS:

Write the definition of intimate.

Using the definition, create a single-sentence prayer about how you would like to have more of this intimacy with God. (Example: Lord, I want to become very familiar with You…)

What does it mean to be real?

Describe what you think it would be like to be real with God.

Write Psalm 18:19 from the Passion Translation.

"There are times in life when we come to the end of ourselves. With nowhere to go, nowhere to turn, we feel a kind of stirring deep inside, and somehow we know that _____ is the only way to find the next _____. In the face of my pain, I had to have the 'real.' My hidden journey _____ closeness with God. That's when the vision came. I saw where He was bringing me—to the broad place. The broad place would be like nothing I had ever known. God and _____. He was the door. I could feel a newness of intimacy with the nature of God."

We are using the fill-in-the-blanks questions to focus on specific points. What does the broad place mean to you in your life?

READ PARAGRAPHS 10-12 AND ANSWER THE FOLLOWING:

"God has invited every one of us to come into His presence with confidence and _____ Him—our all-knowing, all-seeing, ever-present, miraculous God. Knowing God more intimately develops your_____ and _____ of your_____. The miraculous God connects with the miraculous you. He pulls on the miraculous you and leads you into a miraculous life with Him. Knowing Him more intimately automatically pulls you into the realm of _____, and _____ because those are things He does, and you are His partner. Whether you are a relatively new believer or a very seasoned believer—there is _____, _____ intimacy with God. God's miraculous world is without limit!"

In response to the above paragraph, describe your desire for having the "always more" of God.

What do you think a life of greater signs, wonders, and miracles would look like? In what ways do you have this in your life right now?

INTIMACY WITH THE NATURE OF GOD

How would you explain the difference between reading an instruction book on how to pray and learning from experience? What are some of the unique benefits of each learning method?

Describe your closeness with God. Where are you now and where do you want to be?

"As my relationship with God the Father began to deepen and grow, and _____ developed between us, I learned that He also wanted to be _____. He wanted to _____ with me. He _____ me He _____ me."

In your own way, describe intimacy with God.

Write Psalm 63:6-8 from the Passion Translation.

READ PARAGRAPHS 13 TO 21 AND RESPOND TO THE FOLLOWING:

"There is no formula for how to draw closer to God. It is a real_____. You have your own special, personal relationship with God and your own _____ way of knowing Him more_____."

It can be hard to put words to our relationship with God. How would you best describe your own personal relationship with God?

You have your own unique and very special intimacy with God. Describe what it is like for you to be intimate with God. How does it feel? What kinds of things do you say? What is it like to be quiet with Him? What do you see? Listen. What do you hear? Is there a fragrance?

When you turn your attention to God, what is the longing of your heart? Close your eyes and ask, "What is the cry of my heart?" Write a statement that represents the cry of your heart.

In Revelation 3:20, Jesus states that if you hear His voice and open the door, He will come in and eat with you, and you will eat with Him. Eating together really means intimate fellowship. Knowing this, what does this verse mean to you? What action can you take?

Write out Jeremiah 29:13.

"Intimacy with God is available to every believer, including YOU. He said it Himself; God is calling us to _____with Him."

To develop a closer relationship with God, you have to make room for Him. In what ways do you set aside time for God?

What can you do right now to give God your most important commodity: your time?

"You have access to God 24/7. Simply _____ in Him just as you would a close friend. You tell Him _____, and He tells you _____. That's what close friends do. They share the intimate secrets of their hearts."

As you continue with this course, tell Him your secrets. Then listen. In the Passion Translation, Proverbs 3:32b reads, *"...but every tender lover finds friendship with God and will hear his intimate secrets."*

POSTURING INSIGHTS: Read through the Posturing Declarations Out Loud with the Next Question in Mind.

Choose three verses that are hard for you to speak or believe. Write them here.

It can be hard for us to believe that God desires a close, even intimate relationship with us. But He does. Whether your desire to be closer to God is at the beginning stages or if you are already finding that you are super close to Him, there is always more. Just like with a real close relationship with a person grows, you can keep developing an ever-deeper closeness with God.

This is not meant to be an opportunity for you to be hard on yourself if you do not know how to pursue God or if you have not thought about it very much. The point is, He is drawing you into more profound experiences with Him. Ask the Holy Spirit about why you are challenged by these verses. Ask Him to reveal what you have told yourself rather than believing what is written in the verse. Be real. The very thought you have chosen to believe is a *lie*. You ask, *"Why is it a lie?"* Because it is contrary to what God says is true about you. It is a false belief that is negative and limiting you from being who God created you to be. Write down the lies as you see them.

Lies are spiritual strongholds in our minds. Replacing lies with truth is how we pull down strongholds and dismantle lies. The New Testament describes this process in 2 Corinthians 10:4-5 (NKJV):

> *"For the weapons of our warfare are not carnal but mighty in God for pulling down strongholds, casting down arguments and every high thing that exalts itself against the knowledge of God,* **bringing every thought** *into captivity to the obedience of Christ."*

In other words, we pull down and remove every *thought* that is not in agreement with who God is and who He says we are, and we replace it with what is true.

A helpful part of the process is for you to break the agreement you have had with the lie. Praying is the place to start. Right now, you can break the agreement you have had. Pray,

"God, I'm really sorry for believing a lie. I see it now, and I believe the truth of Your Word. Right now, I break the agreement I have had with this lie. Forgive me. Heal the hurt place in my heart where the lie came into my life. Fill my heart and mind with Your truth as I speak Your Word, in Jesus' name, Amen."

Every one of us has bought into wrong beliefs and mindsets. Are you surprised to realize there are lies you have adhered to? Include your response to this process.

EXPERIENTIAL ACTIVATIONS: Unveiling Your Hidden Journey

ACTIVATION ONE

Aligning yourself with God is proactively joining the adventure of *unveiling your hidden journey*. Alignment of your true self with who God says you are is paramount. Speaking posturing declarations is the most important activation you can do in the entire study of your *Miraculous Identity*. I want to clarify what I mean. By "*posture*" I mean to take a stand, to position yourself, to purposefully assume a posture of declaring to the atmosphere on earth and to the heavens who God really is and who you really are—your *miraculous identity*. Personalizing verses enables you to own them. They become part of you. Posturing in declarations is to become an intentional speaker. You get hold of a verse that is personalized, speak it, and then stand in faith for the fullness of the verse to saturate your entire being. Our focus is intimacy with God. This is a great verse:

> *"With passion I pursue and cling to you. Because I feel your grip on my life, I keep my soul close to your heart"* (Psalm 63:8).

Immerse yourself in Intimacy with the Nature of God. Let the posturing declarations drop down into your spirit. The Word of God is alive and will come alive inside you. The personalized verses will move from your mind down into your spirit, to the place in you where deep calls unto deep.

Speak the verses aloud daily for one week. Tenderly say them out loud two times a day—in the morning and right before bed. Actually, I suggest you have the book with you throughout the day so you can go through the verses frequently. The more you say them, the more they become part of you. This is not the time to be lazy or let things slide. This is your time, your valuable set-apart time to really align yourself with your true, miraculous identity. This study is *for* you. You will be transformed because of the words you speak. You can speak either life or death. These declarations are *life*. I encourage you to grab hold of the hem of His garment and press in to God's presence in your life.

After one week, choose ten of the personalized verses and highlight them in your book to continue to speak once a day for at least thirty days.

Increased revelation of intimacy with God will start to become a part of you. Renewing your mind is an action you do intentionally, and this week you are purposefully going after intimacy with God. In doing so, you dismantle opposing mental strongholds. You are proclaiming revelation to the atmosphere around you and within you. You are a warrior. A pursuer. Diligent. Valiant. Dangerous. The dreaded champion. Going deeper. Going further. May a profound hunger stir inside you.

One-Week Verse Recitations Check-Off List (all 51)

Day	Sunday	Monday	Tuesday	Wednesday	Thursday	Friday	Saturday
Morning							
Bedtime							

Thirty-Day Verse Recitations Check-Off List (10 favorites)

<u>Verse</u> day	1	2	3	4	5	6	7	8	9	10
1										
2										
3										
4										
5										
6										
7										
8										
9										
10										
11										
12										
13										
14										
15										
16										
17										
18										
19										

20									
21									
22									
23									
24									
25									
26									
27									
28									
29									
30									

Describe the reaction of your inner spirit to these verse recitations.

ACTIVATION TWO

God's love for us is so vast, so deep, and so wide, and He invites us into that love daily. Sometimes it's easy to run into His loving arms and spend time with Him; sometimes it's difficult. As you posture, you may find difficulty fully embracing the reality of a close, personal relationship with God. You may be thinking that you don't pray enough or that you don't know the Bible enough. You may think that with the things you've done and the mistakes you've made, this kind of closeness with God isn't available to you. You may think you are not worthy to come into God's presence. There may be a deep place in you where you feel that you are not important. These are lies. Guess who doesn't want you to become closer with the God of the universe?

When anyone draws near to God, God draws near to him. No one is excluded. Look at James 4:7 from a few translations. Here are two:

"Move your heart closer to God, and he will come even closer to you." (Passion Translation)

"Draw near to God and He will draw near to you." (NKJV)

This activation is simple but will stay with you all week. Write this verse on paper or post-its and place it on the bathroom mirror, on your refrigerator, on your car dashboard, and anywhere else you frequent. When you see it, ponder it and decree it.

ACTIVATION THREE

Find a quiet place where you can sit and have some alone time with God. This can be a corner of your backyard, the car, or a walk-in closet. A place where you will be undisturbed. Bring a Bible and a notebook you can begin using regularly to record your God-experiences.

Wait and listen. If you are not feeling much, it's okay. Continue to practice being in His presence. If you lack a strong desire to know Him and spend time with Him, simply ask for that desire.

Ask Him to tell you what is on His heart. Tell Him what is on your heart. Go back and forth, learning to listen and freely talk to God. Write down what you are sensing. God speaks to us in many different ways. You may get a picture, a phrase, a word, a revelation about something on your heart. He will speak to you through His Word. Sometimes, we just "know" what He is telling us. That's all we can say to describe it—it is a knowing.

Write your experience with God.

ACTIVATION FOUR

Play worship music that really moves you, and sit completely still, with your eyes closed, focusing everything within you on Him alone. Then, after a bit, turn off the music to be even more fully engaged with Him. This way you will not follow the words or the beat of the music. You are still before Him. Ask Him to reveal Himself to you. Ask anything about your life. Ask anything about anything. Being intimate means you are seeing into one another.

Get started with these questions:

Lord, what do You want to be for me?

Lord, what is the next thing You want to heal in me?

Have fun with your imagination! Draw a picture of what it might look like to have God drawing near to you as you draw near to Him. I love doing this. I get out crayons and colored, felt-tipped pens and draw like a third-grader, and I know He loves it.

PRAYER FOCUS: Intimacy with the Nature of God

Read the Intimacy prayer. Expand it and make it more your own by adding some your thoughts to the prayer. Write it here.

HEAVENLY WORD

The love God has for you is so extreme, so passionate, so extravagant! Song of Songs aptly describes His love for you. Read through the heavenly word and look up the verses from Song of Songs that are listed below it. Write down phrases and words that stand out to you.

Video Notes

2
The Secret Place
Meeting with God

You have an invitation to dwell in the secret place of the Most High. Here you are safe. Hidden. Secure. Here the troubles of this world cannot overcome you, because you are in Him. The secret place is a refuge. For you. Regardless of your circumstances, you can find Jesus resting in the boat. You too can lie down with Him and rest in your storm. This is His promise to us. This is part of your *miraculous identity*. Part of your *hidden journey* with God. We truly find refuge under the shadow of His wings. As you read this chapter and answer these questions, let God's protection and security permeate your entire being. Step into the glory of the Lord. Find knowledge and revelation and deep friendship with Him. He is your defender, your protector, and your refuge. He is your Secret Place.

He who dwells in the secret place of the Most High
shall abide under the shadow of the Almighty.
PSALM 91:1

READ PARAGRAPHS ONE AND TWO.

"The secret place of the Most High is _____ _____."

The beauty of the secret place is that it is a _____,
_____, a realm in the spirit where you _____
_____, safely tucked away from the world's strife."

What does refuge mean, and how is God your refuge?

"It is a place where you can hear heaven's songs and enjoy _____ _____ with God. It is here that you find _____ for your soul, where your spirit is _____, and where your body is _____ _____."

In the secret place of the Most High, you are a _____, and you are a _____."

According to the teaching, what does a lover/warrior do?

Share an example of someone in the Bible who pursued God like a lover and a warrior.

"The combination of lover/warrior makes you wild and unpredictable in the eyes of the world because you do _____ _____.

You aren't led by _____ or swayed by man.

You walk to the _____ of heaven."

Worldly definitions of rhythm include words like flow, pulse, cadence, tempo, vibration, harmony, magnificence, and gracefulness. Antonyms include disagreement, discord, imbalance, crudeness, and unimportance. Consider these definitions. What would you say it means to walk in the rhythm of heaven?

READ PARAGRAPHS THREE AND FOUR AND ANSWER THE FOLLOWING QUESTIONS.

"When you spend time with God, _____ _____ _____. In His presence, you are _____ _____."

How have your thoughts and actions changed since you began getting closer to God?

"As you saturate yourself in His presence, _____ _____ and invisible prisons that held you captive are weakened and dissolved, floating away downstream. You are _____ and _____ _____ in the secret place of the Most High."

Read Matthew 11:28-30. What does God remove from us?

A great exchange takes place in the secret place. What does He give us in exchange for our heavy yoke?

What is the most recent yoke God showed you and then removed from you?

Are there any burdens on your heart right now? Close your eyes, take a deep breath, and give them to Jesus. He will lift the weight of them from you and replace them with His peace and His presence. Okay, who can draw like a third-grader? Time to get out the colored pens and crayons! It is really interesting to have a visual for this. Draw the old, burdensome yoke and the new easy yoke.

"As you are healed and refreshed, it is natural to become filled with His _____ ___ _____."

"A desire grows to learn what is on _____ _____."

What grows and enlarges as you spend time in the secret place?

Looking back over the chapter, what takes place inside us as we spend time in the secret place?

READ PARAGRAPHS FIVE, SIX, AND SEVEN.

What does the word "know" mean?

"_____ is present when you are deep in the secret place of the Most High."

POSTURING INSIGHTS: Read through the Posturing Declarations Out Loud with the Next Question in Mind.

We throw open our doors to God and discover at the same moment he has already thrown open his door to us We find ourselves standing where we always hoped we might stand—out in the wide open spaces of God's grace and glory, standing tall and shouting our praise (Romans 5:2 The Message).

We open the door and find He is already there! God is relentless. He continually draws you into His secret place, the secret place of His presence. You long to go there with Him, but maybe you've had a hard time drawing close when you postured in the verses. If any of the verses were difficult for you to believe, choose a few of them and write them down.

Then, ask God to show you why you had a hard time believing them. When we have a hard time believing God, we have undoubtedly believed a lie—something in opposition to what God has said. Remember how the serpent got Eve to question God and believe a lie? The serpent said to Eve, *"Did God really say…?"* (Genesis 3:1).

Ask God to show you the lie you have adopted in place of the truth of the verse. Write the lie here.

Once you see the lie, quiet your heart and ask God to forgive you for believing the lie. Write about this here.

Next, verbally break the agreement you have had with the lie. Say, *"Lord, I am sorry for believing the lie. It kept me from believing Your Word. In Jesus' Name, I break my agreement with that lie. The bondage is broken! From now on, I believe. …"* Say the verse again in your own words. Write what is new and real and true for you here.

Now take some time let God heal any place in your heart was affected by the lie. Say, *"Lord, heal the injured place in my heart when the lie came in."* Ask Him to show you or reveal anything you need to know concerning the lie. Share this here.

Be real. Be transparent. Know that He draws you close as He heals your heart. God is continually interacting with you. He draws you, gives you revelation, and transforms you—continually. As you go through *Miraculous You*, more and more you will recognize how God is always engaged with you. And your sensitivity to the Spirit of God will expand. That is where we will go in the next chapter. It is going to be awesome!

EXPERIENTIAL ACTIVATIONS: ENTERING THE SECRET PLACE

ACTIVATION ONE

That you are reading this book indicates you are not willing to settle for a superficial relationship with God. You want more. The desire inside you causes you to become militant and to aggressively pursue God. Miraculous identity means being miraculously close to God, and through deep relationship with Him you enter into the secret place.

Read the personalized verses twice a day—first thing in the morning and right before bed. Then, after one week, choose ten verses to continue to proclaim for the next thirty days. This is not a religious exercise. You are proactively renewing your mind. This requires discipline. And, yes, sometimes you may not feel like doing it. Do it anyway. Develop perseverance. Give your passion and strength into seeking Him (Hebrews 11:6). I suggest you write them out or start a posturing file on your computer and rotate the ten verses.

I encourage you. You've got this. You are developing a habit, a lifestyle.

One-Week Verse Recitations Check-Off List (all 47)

Day	Sunday	Monday	Tuesday	Wednesday	Thursday	Friday	Saturday
Morning							
Bedtime							

Thirty-Day Verse Recitations Check-Off List (10 favorites)

Verse / day	1	2	3	4	5	6	7	8	9	10
1										
2										
3										
4										
5										
6										
7										
8										
9										
10										
11										
12										
13										
14										
15										
16										
17										
18										
19										
20										
21										
22										
23										
24										

25								
26								
27								
28								
29								
30								

Describe the reaction of your inner spirit to these verse recitations.

ACTIVATION TWO

Activation two is a very experiential activation for entering in and being in the secret place of the Most High. The secret place can be a physical location you go to meet with God, but it most often connotes a state of your soul in relationship with God. We meet with Him in the secret places of the heart. Here, we commune with Him—transparent and honest. Matthew 6:6 offers a great description:

> *When you pray, go into your room, and when you have shut your door, pray to your Father who is in the secret place; and your Father who sees in secret will reward you openly.*

After posturing in the secret place verses, think about your secret place as being within you. Close your eyes and focus on a place deep within the core of your being. Posture in that inner place and spend time with God. Keep it simple. Just be quiet and relax there. Relax your whole self into this place of solitude with Him. Watch and see if you can feel His presence there.

You can enter the secret place anytime and anywhere. As a prophetic symbol, create a secret place in your house. It can be a room, a chair, a closet, on the patio, or even in your car. Do something to create an atmosphere. For example, you can use pillows, a cozy blanket, or candles. The point is to create a relaxing, peaceful atmosphere and enter in with purpose.

Take the Bible with you. Take worship music. Take a notepad. Focus your heart and mind to enter into the Lord's presence. Tenderly, say some of the personalized posturing verses. Ultimately, become completely quiet and still. Don't move. Say, *"Holy, Holy, Holy are You Lord,"* for as long as you feel. Sense the Holy Spirit's presence. Whisper posturing words. Your own words. Read passages of the Bible that you love.

This is an activation to use as a tool to help you get there. It is not a formula or a set-in-stone, how-to method. We are just getting the train on the track or priming the pump. If possible, do this every day for the week you are focusing on the secret place. Rise early, if you must. Then, with Holy Spirit, enter into the secret place in your own personal, individual way. Your special, unique way with God.

Write about your experience.

ACTIVATION THREE

When you are in the secret place, you posture yourself from where you are truly seated—where God raised you up with Christ and seated you with Him in the heavenly realms far above all rule and authority, power and dominion and every negative manifestation (Ephesians 1:20-23; 2:6). Wow! Yep, that's you.

Think of a circumstance that is trying to stir up a storm in your life. Declare to it that you are seated in heavenly realms with Christ Jesus. Really ponder this truth.

Rewrite these verses from Ephesians in your own words.

Speak to your challenging situation using words from these verses. These verses reflect the secret place. Pull them in close to the inner secret place in your belly. From your belly—which is the same as your innermost being—is the place from which rivers of living waters flow! Now think about that. Close your eyes and sense the rivers of living waters (John 7:38). Look up this verse, then close your eyes and focus on this truth. Really ponder it. Listen to me. Don't hurry back to your activities. This is your time. Give God your most valuable commodity: your time.

ACTIVATION FOUR

The dictionary defines *refuge* as a condition of being safe or sheltered from pursuit, danger or trouble. If you look it up in Strong's Concordance (#4268), you will see it defined as a shelter (literally or figuratively) —hope, place of refuge, shelter, and trust.

In a childlike way, draw a picture of the secret place—your place of refuge. Be like a child and draw outside the lines. In other words: Don't think you have to create a perfect work of art. Draw from your heart. God loves this about you! He loves the expressions of your heart. What are the colors? Are there sounds? Is there a fragrance? What is the atmosphere like?

PRAYER FOCUS: Entering the Secret Place

Add some more lines of your own to the prayer.

HEAVENLY WORD

Look up the Scripture references written below the Heavenly Word. Write key words that stand out to you personally.

Video Notes

3
The Wind of the Spirit

His Name is the Spirit of Truth ... He is the Revealer

The Holy Spirit knows everything you ever need to know. He has a grand sense of humor and great wisdom. The adventure you are on with Him can be called *"Life Interrupted!,"* because He will interrupt what you are doing and present a wondrous opportunity to you. He pulls you into God's miraculous world of signs, wonders, and miracles. He gives you dreams that are way beyond your ability. To achieve these dreams, you will need Him. And that's all right with Him—He loves doing things with you. He loves being with you. He loves being your Partner! Every day, you grow closer to the Holy Spirit. In this study, you are growing closer *intentionally*.

READ PARAGRAPHS ONE TO SIX.

The Holy Spirit is like the _____. When the _____ blows, you can't _____ it.

"The wind blows wherever it pleases. You hear its sound, but you cannot tell where it comes from or where it is going. So it is with everyone born of the Spirit" (John 3:8). In your own words, how is the Holy Spirit like the wind?

Most of us like to be in control. Here is a key: Thinking you have a better way all on your own is pride. In essence you are saying, "I've got this. I don't need You. I can do this on my own." As we develop our relationship with Holy Spirit, we practice yielding to Him. He is our Partner, our Helper, and our Counselor. He has grand ideas. Ginormous ideas. And He knows how you and He together can accomplish them. He knows how to help you navigate through troubled waters. Dream big, and with Him, you will dream bigger. Think big and prepare to think bigger.

Why is life yielded to the Holy Spirit more fulfilling than independence?

Why do you think yielding to Him can be hard?

On a scale from 1 to 10, with 10 being the highest awareness of the Holy Spirit, how conscious do you think you are of the presence of the Holy Spirit right now in your life? Why?

Whatever your answer is, it's okay. You are not going to stay there! You are *transforming* and growing closer with every breath. You can engage in conversation with Him. Maybe you talk with Him a lot already. Right now, what would you like to say to Holy Spirit?

READ PARAGRAPH SEVEN.

We are not to be ruled by _____. Following externals—circumstances and our own ideas about how we can make our futures work out—causes us to be _____ _____.

It produces _____ and _____. The Holy Spirit's plan does not include this kind of _____.

The Bible speaks of wind, breath, and Spirit in reference to the Holy Spirit. What if the wind were blowing *inside* my house? I'd see papers flying, vases falling over, chandeliers swinging sideways. What if this wind blew inside *me*? What would that feel like? Would everything in me fall into alignment with His purposes? Would He blow out all the unhealed places? Would He breathe life into my dreams and visions? Would I be filled with the breath of heaven? You bet. Close your eyes and pause right now. Focus on the wind of the Spirit within you. Can you feel that? Step into God's world of color and sound and vision. Describe what you see and feel.

Read through the teaching section of this chapter and highlight or underline everything that stands out to you. What three points stand out to you the most and why?

Look up Acts 15:28 and consider the close relationship we can have with the Holy Spirit. The Holy Spirit gives us ideas, and then He prompts us to act on those ideas. Close your eyes and ask the Holy Spirit to show you an idea He has been stirring in you. What is the idea?

What is He prompting you to do with this idea? If you don't know yet, ask Him right now. Activate this idea by asking Him, "What is my next step with this idea?"

POSTURING INSIGHTS: Read through the Posturing Declarations Out Loud with the Next Question in Mind.

What verses do you feel challenged believing and grabbing hold of? Write down three of them here.

Your relationship with the Holy Spirit is very personal and unique to you. He knows how to reach you. He knows everything about you. He knows your past, is involved with your present, and sees what lies ahead of you. As you learn about what He is like, you may have difficulty believing everything about Him. He is real. Just as real as the Father and just as real as Jesus. It is easier for people to believe in the Father because they can picture Him. People can believe in Jesus because He walked the earth. But Holy Spirit? How do we think of Him?

Look at the verses and ask, "What have I believed that keeps me from believing this verse? Write your thoughts here.

When your thoughts/beliefs are contrary, a lie is revealed. It is time to dismantle that lie. Lies hold a place in our intellect until we cast them down. Just like in previous chapters, break your agreement with the lie. Talk to God right now and proclaim the truth you choose to believe about Holy Spirit.

EXPERIENTIAL ACTIVATIONS: Yielding to the Wind of the Spirit

ACTIVATION ONE

Posturing in *Holy Spirit, I Want to Know You!* will plant key verses about the Holy Spirit in your heart, enabling an increased awareness of His presence. Understanding the nature of Holy Spirit, what He does, and how He functions as part of the Trinity affects your ability to recognize the many ways He relates to you throughout the day.

Personal note: I'm so used to Him being referred to as "the" Holy Spirit that I do this often myself. But then, because He is a person, I will also refer to Him directly as Holy Spirit. I use these ways of addressing Him interchangeably.

For this activation, your assignment is to proclaim these verses for one week—first thing in the morning when you get up and right before you go to bed. After one week of posturing twice a day, choose ten verses to speak once a day for thirty days. Continuing this lifestyle of proclaiming God's Word allows the truths to continue to renew your mind, drop down into your spirit, and ultimately become a vibrant facet of your miraculous identity.

One-Week Verse Recitations Check-Off List (all 38)

Day	Sunday	Monday	Tuesday	Wednesday	Thursday	Friday	Saturday
Morning							
Bedtime							

Thirty-Day Verse Recitations Check-Off List (10 favorites)

Verse/day	1	2	3	4	5	6	7	8	9	10
1										
2										
3										
4										
5										
6										
7										
8										
9										
10										
11										
12										

13										
14										
15										
16										
17										
18										
19										
20										
21										
22										
23										
24										
25										
26										
27										
28										
29										
30										

What three verses affect you the most powerfully?

Why are these verses so important to you right now?

Consider your growing intimacy with the Holy Spirit. What additional Holy Spirit-related verses would you like to add as posturing statements of your own?

Track your posturing here with a check mark:

Day	Sunday	Monday	Tuesday	Wednesday	Thursday	Friday	Saturday
Morning							
Bedtime							

Describe the reaction of your inner spirit to these verse recitations.

When I became a Christian, I wanted to learn everything I could about Holy Spirit. I came out of the new age movement and, after so much deception, I fervently wanted to know the Spirit of Truth. Since the book of Acts reveals the power of the Spirit in the early church (Acts 1:8), I read through Acts and marked every time the Holy Spirit is mentioned or when His power is demonstrated.

This is the second part of Activation One: Read through Acts. Mark an "S" in your Bible every time there is a demonstration of the Holy Spirit. Your eyes will be opened to how intimately early church believers knew Holy Spirit. He was so real to them. Regarding an idea they had, they said, "Holy Spirit and we thought it was a good idea!"

ACTIVATION TWO

Fasten your seatbelts, I am going to share something very important! What I am about to say might sound like it is contrary to the emphasis in this book on proclaiming verses about miraculous identity—but it is not. When you are in the throes of transition and transformation and are going through a very difficult passage, God is right there with you. He is holding you up and sustaining you. It was in the midst of extremely difficult seasons of loss, betrayal, and severe anxiety that I learned what I am about to tell you. When you understand this, you enter His rest.

During many transitional seasons of your life, know this: *You can't proclaim your way through it. He carries you through it.*

This passage exemplifies this truth:

> *Are you tired? Worn out? Burned out on religion? Come to me. Get away with me and you'll recover your life. I'll show you how to take a real rest. Walk with me and work with me—watch how I do it. Learn the unforced rhythms of grace. I won't lay anything heavy or ill-fitting on you. Keep company with me and you'll learn to live freely and lightly* (Matthew 11:28-30 The Message)

As you go through this book, I don't want you to feel that proclaiming verses is a weight on your shoulders. It is not. I command that concept to lift off your shoulders right now, in Jesus' name. Proclaiming verses renews your mind and aligns your thought-life identity with how heaven sees you. You are simply adhering to Romans 12:1-2, and as you do so, God Almighty does the unseen, inner transformative work deep within you.

In this activation, you will practice connecting to the place inside you where deep calls unto deep and rivers of living waters spring forth. Right now, pray out loud in the Spirit (Jude 1:20) and think about praying in your head. Concentrate on hearing your voice in your head.

After about a minute, pray in the Spirit and focus on your mouth. Think about the sounds of the words in your mouth.

Now, you will go to the headwaters of the Holy Spirit. Drop your focus down to deep within your belly and pray in the Spirit from there. Keep going. Think about how Jesus said rivers of living waters will flow from deep within your belly. Stay here for a while. Think about how rivers coming together churn and stir and are vibrant with great force.

Do this activation as part of your prayer time throughout the week. Write your experience.

ACTIVATION THREE

The third activation is an outdoor adventure. Go outside and experience the movement of the wind. There may be a gentle breeze or a super strong wind blowing. Most often it is barely a whisper of movement. Ask Holy Spirit to teach you about how He moves by watching the movement of the natural wind. Watch how everything moves in the wind. How does the wind feel on your face? Now focus your attention of the wind moving inside you. What is He doing inside you? Share your insights.

ACTIVATION FOUR

During Jesus' final hours before He was arrested and crucified, He taught the disciples about the person of the Holy Spirit. Look at these verses listed below that will tell you more about Holy Spirit. Next to the verse, make some notes of what they reveal about Holy Spirit? Write

John 14:15-18, 25-26

John 15:25-27

John 16:12-14

Acts 1;1-2, 1:8

Acts 2

PRAYER FOCUS: Led by the Spirit

Read the Led by the Spirit Prayer Focus in the book. What part of this prayer impacts you the most?

In your life right now, where do you see the Holy Spirit partnering with you?

What does it mean to have Him as your partner?

HEAVENLY WORD

Read the Heavenly Word in the book. Holy Spirit is your best friend, your Revealer and Guide. Close your eyes and ask Him to show you how He is involved in your life. Write down here what you feel He is showing you.

Video Notes

Humility
Bowing Low

The seat of humility within you is a tender and vulnerable place of your hidden journey. Only you can choose to discover the fruit and life of humility. Your miraculous identity contains true humility. True humility says, "God, I need You. I know only so much. I can do only so much. I honor You and humble myself before You. I surrender my life to You." Material abundance often detracts from inner wealth, particularly from the riches of humility. Humility is the receptacle and engine for learning. We cannot learn what we're too proud to admit we do not know. Do you want humility? Humility is demonstrated outwardly from an inner, hidden transformation taking place because of a renewed mind.

From the above section, begin to position your heart with how true humility prays. What does the final sentence say to you?

Write the definition of humble.

REFER TO THE TEACHING SECTION IN THE BOOK AND ANSWER THE FOLLOWING QUESTIONS:

"It's not on your shoulders to make things happen. You don't have to figure everything out. Just breathe. Let go. You have a partner. … Humility is yielding to His lead." We see these statements in the first paragraph of chapter 4.

Explain why yielding to God's lead is a key form of humility.

What are some practical ways one might yield to God's leading?

List an example of a time you yielded to God's leading and how doing so affected your life.

"The truth is, you cannot accomplish anything of eternal significance without Him. Period. Humility before the Lord is recognizing you need God's help."

List at least one biblical character who sought to accomplish something of eternal significance apart from God—and the result.

List at least one biblical character who sought to accomplish something of eternal significance through God—and the result.

As you consider your legacy, which of those two biblical characters will you commit to emulate? How do you see that affecting your legacy?

Referring to paragraph five, what concepts stand out to you, minister to you or encourage you? Explain why the Holy Spirit is crucial to your humble accomplishments.

Romans 12:1 exemplifies humility before God. The Passion Translation reads: "Beloved friends, what should be our proper response to God's marvelous mercies? I encourage you to surrender yourselves to God to be his sacred, living sacrifices. And live in holiness, experiencing all that delights his heart. For this becomes your genuine expression of worship."

How does one surrender himself/herself to God?

"With humility permeating your life, your dreams are compelled to bow low before Him." Explain this concept in your own words.

First Peter 5:5 says "God opposes the proud." Why don't we always see that truth in "real time"? Why does it sometimes seem that the humble struggle while the proud prosper under God's favor? (Hint: consider the final words in verse 6.)

"Humility begins to assume the posture of a servant. We are not here on earth to be served but to serve." Think of someone you know who has given his or her life to selflessly serving others.

What is that person's demeanor?

How does that person react to setbacks and difficult circumstances?

"In their book, *Words Can Change Your Brain,* they [Andrew Newberg, M.D. and Mark Robert Waldman] write: 'a single word has the power to influence the expression of genes that regulate physical and emotional stress.'"[1] Words are powerful. Life and death are in the power of the tongue. With the words you speak, you choose life or death.

How might reciting the declarations influence your life?

---

[1] "Words Can Change Your Brain," https://psychcentral.com/blog/words-can-change-your-brain/

POSTURING INSIGHTS: Read through the Posturing Declarations Out Loud with the Next Question in Mind.

Write three verses you either do not believe or have difficulty believing.

Ever read the list of the fruit of the Spirit? Love, joy, peace patience, kindness, goodness, faithfulness, gentleness, and self-control. I see humility woven into every one of these. Struggling with any of these (and I would venture to say all of us do!) is a good indicator of a humility deficit. So, let's go deeper with humility. Look at the verses and ask, "What is it I am believing that keeps me from believing what God presents to me?" Write your response here.

You can dismantle the mindset that keeps you from humility. Yes, it is a stronghold in your mind that hinders you and the growth of love, joy, peace, and all the rest of the fruit of the Spirit. It is time to break free and align your mind with heaven. Go ahead and pray,

"Lord, I want humility to blossom in my life. I choose humility. I'm really sorry for believing a lie that has hindered me from having a more humble heart. I believe the truth of Your Word. Right now, I break the agreement I have had with this lie. Forgive me. Heal the hurt place in my heart where the lie came into my life. Fill my heart and mind with Your truth as I speak Your Word, in Jesus' name, Amen."

This prayer holds power, and in speaking it you will begin to see change in your life. Keep choosing humility. Keep declaring humility. How are you feeling and what are you thinking?

EXPERIENTIAL ACTIVATIONS: HUMILITY—LIVING UNDER THE INFLUENCE OF GOD

ACTIVATION ONE

Now you are familiar with the foremost activation—daily posturing. I simply cannot stress enough the need to be proactive in renewing your mind. God does not do this for you. YOU do it. You are the one who renews your mind. Not Him. Renewing your mind places the caterpillar in the cocoon. Then, while in the cocoon, the Holy Spirit can perform the miraculous transformation of your identity. Yes, the butterfly is you. Transformation is not a one-time event. Every facet of your miraculous identity goes into the cocoon. This is a huge key: it starts with your mind. Renewing your mind. Aligning your thoughts with what God says is true about you. What you do is come into agreement with God.

Proclaim the humility verses for one week, first thing in the morning when you get up, and right before you go to bed. Then, choose ten verses to speak at least once a day for thirty days. These truths will renew your mind and drop down into your spirit and become part of you.

One-Week Verse Recitations Check-Off List (all 26)

Day	Sunday	Monday	Tuesday	Wednesday	Thursday	Friday	Saturday
Morning							
Bedtime							

Thirty-Day Verse Recitations Check-Off List (10 favorites)

Verse/Day	1	2	3	4	5	6	7	8	9	10
1										
2										
3										
4										
5										
6										

7											
8											
9											
10											
11											
12											
13											
14											
15											
16											
17											
18											
19											
20											
21											
22											
23											
24											
25											
26											
27											
28											
29											
30											

Describe the reaction of your inner spirit to these verse recitations.

Pride may come to discourage you, to keep you from binding yourself to humility. Right now, I see these verses like post-its all over your body. Do you sense what is happening? The word is life to you. God's word to Joshua (Joshua 1:8) was to "meditate on it day and night."

What three verses affect you the most powerfully?

Why are these verses so important to you right now?

Consider your growing intimacy with the Holy Spirit. What additional verses would you like to add as posturing statements of your own?

ACTIVATION TWO

Play anointed worship music that really ministers to your heart, and "lay low" before God. Put your body in a few different positions as you present your body as a living sacrifice before the Lord. Try stretching out flat on the floor and kneeling and bowing before Him. Posture your heart as you posture your body. Use some of the posturing verses with which you feel strongly connected and say them to the Lover of your soul. You can even meditate on what it means for you to be a living sacrifice. Really enjoy this. This is your time. Just you and your Creator.

ACTIVATION THREE

In Acts 20:19, Paul said he was "serving the Lord with all humility." Google/look-up the meaning of humility. What does this word mean to you? Think of someone who exemplifies humility. How do you see humility demonstrated in this person's character? How is humility at work in your life?

ACTIVATION FOUR

Jesus came "not to be served, but to serve and give His life as a ransom for many." Every day, we wash the feet of others when we serve and minister to them. Today, ask God for opportunities to demonstrate His heart of love and compassion toward people through simple acts of kindness. Want some ideas? Give out bottles of water. Smile. Tell somebody what a great job they are doing. I will often say, "Would you be offended if I prayed for you?" By asking permission, I have rarely been turned down. I tell them to close their eyes, and I pray a blessing over their lives. Or for whatever they need. It might be a need for healing in the body or heart, a better job, peace instead of anxiety, a closer walk with God. You get the idea.

PRAYER FOCUS: Humility

This humility prayer in the book is only a starting place for you. Re-write the prayer the way you want to say it.

HEAVENLY WORD

What impacts you the most in the Heavenly Word?

Video Notes

5
Supernaturally Faithful
The Game Changer

David's life was full of great tests and trials. He was nearly killed many times. Friends turned on him. David wandered in the wilderness, hiding in caves, alone and rejected. Yet he was able to make this profound statement in Psalm 35:27: *"I was young and now I am old, yet I have never seen the righteous forsaken."* That's a stunning revelation from a man who did not live an easy life. He must have known a secret. He knew that no matter what, God is *faithful*. He knew that no matter the circumstance, God is good. We must learn this truth as well. It's time to move past our circumstances into God's reality, where He is good and loving and absolutely faithful!

READ PARAGRAPHS ONE THROUGH FOUR

Looking at the definition, to be faithful means to be _____, _____ _____. When you think of the word "faithful" what other words or pictures come to mind?

God's faithfulness is unlike anything else. He is completely faithful. His faithfulness reaches to the skies! God's faithfulness is supernatural—no one can match His faithfulness. Stop and think about it. How is He *miraculously* faithful to YOU?

Trusting God in the midst of great loss can be very challenging. Have you had to lean on God during a hard time in your own life? Share how He carried you through a difficult circumstance.

READ PARAGRAPHS FIVE AND SIX

"God is faithful to do what He says He will do. He is faithful to His Word. His very nature and character are unchanging. He fulfills all His wonderful promises. He promises he will take care of you."

What promises contained in Psalm 23 (shared in paragraph five) are most meaningful to you?

Believing God is _____ to guide you, help you, and love you is paramount to your faith.

What name did God use to introduce Himself? _____

Choosing to believe that *He is,* while you are staring at the uncertainty of the future, compels you to acknowledge that God relentlessly invades your world with a heavenly reality where anything is possible.

How has God already demonstrated to you that anything is possible?

READ PARAGRAPHS SEVEN THROUGH THIRTEEN AND ANSWER THE FOLLOWING.

When thinking about God's faithfulness, what do most of us think about?
_____

When is it easiest for us to acknowledge His faithfulness?
_____

When is our real faith put to the test?
_____

Knowing He is faithful gives you:
_____

Knowing He has already (past tense) given you hope ("I give you hope and a future," see Jeremiah 29:11) upon which to hang your faith during seemingly hopeless situations is a gamechanger.

What are you standing in faith for in your life right now?

What trap did the Israelites fall into when they were not postured to believe that God was faithful?
_____

What kept the Israelites out of the Promised Land? _____

To the Israelites the Promised Land represented a land of freedom, promise, and abundance. What is your "Promised Land?"

Make up your mind about God _____. Believe _____ in everything the Bible reveals about God's character. Now is the time to _____ in accepting that He is faithful to YOU.

THEN ANSWER THE FOLLOWING QUESTIONS.

Don't wait until you're in the midst of a trial, finding yourself wondering if God's going to come through. How are you building yourself up right now? As you proclaim God's faithfulness, _____
_____!

You will find yourself in the Heavenly Realms with God's _____
_____ inscribed upon your heart.

SUPERNATURALLY FAITHFUL

Posturing is one way to build up your faith in God. What are some ways you have encouraged yourself to stay close to God's faithfulness in the past?

POSTURING INSIGHTS: Read through the Posturing Declarations Out Loud with the Next Question in Mind.

Don't wait until something happens and you are desperate. Pick up these verses. Posture now to prepare yourself for future trials. Declare all of the posturing verses out loud.

Which three verses stand out to you?

Are there any verses you have difficulty saying?

Ask Holy Spirit to reveal the lie you have believed rather than the truth. For example: I think God forgets about me, I am not important enough, or I have a hard time believing God loves me. You have told yourself a falsehood that stands in the way of your believing what God says. What is the lie?

Great. You are making progress! Now, break the agreement with the lie and make the purposeful choice to believe the verse. If you want, look at the prayer in the previous activations.

EXPERIENTIAL ACTIVATIONS: Recognizing His Faithfulness

ACTIVATION ONE

These verses are powerful! Declare them out loud at least twice a day for the next seven days. Also, choose ten verses to continue to proclaim for the next thirty days. Share your experiences below.

One-Week Verse Recitations Check-Off List (all 49)

Day	Sunday	Monday	Tuesday	Wednesday	Thursday	Friday	Saturday
Morning							
Bedtime							

Thirty-Day Verse Recitations Check-Off List (10 favorites)

Verse day	1	2	3	4	5	6	7	8	9	10
1										
2										
3										
4										
5										
6										
7										
8										
9										
10										
11										
12										
13										
14										

15									
16									
17									
18									
19									
20									
21									
22									
23									
24									
25									
26									
27									
28									
29									
30									

Describe the reaction of your inner spirit to these verse recitations.

ACTIVATION TWO

God promises that He will never leave or forsake you (Hebrews 13:5). He has always been right by your side, through thick and thin. Think of a time when you felt God deserted you but later realized He was with you all the time. Often, we see a bigger picture weeks, months, or even years later.

What challenging situation are you facing right now? Yes, God is at work in the middle of your current trial, just as He was in the past.

Close your eyes and tell yourself that God is helping you right now with this situation. To the atmosphere around you, say, *"I know You are helping me with this trial—because You are faithful!"*

As you speak, you choose to take a heavenly perspective and see your obstacle from a posture of faith. Continue to say this throughout the week. Remember: life and death are in the power of the tongue. Speak life.

Why is God's faithfulness a gamechanger?

ACTIVATION THREE

Renewing your mind means coming into agreement with God's unrelenting faithfulness and allowing His faithfulness to become more deeply rooted in your being. Yet God is also calling *you* to be faithful. I often tell those I mentor that God is more concerned with *how* you do what you do than *what* you do. Integrity matters. Being honorable and keeping your word matters. Holding fast to your faith matters. In speaking to the church in Smyrna in Revelation 2:10 (Passion Translation) the Lord says Your faithfulness matters.

> *"...remain faithful to the day you die and I will give you the victor's crown of life."*

Consider the following affirmation:

"I belong to God. He chose me and set me apart to Him. Before the heavens and the earth, I proclaim over my life: God is completely faithful to me! And I choose faithfulness. I, myself, choose to be faithful in all I do."

Ponder this in your heart. Right now, proclaim the words out loud. As you speak, anoint yourself with oil. (Hand lotion will work too. Once I used toothpaste when there was nothing else!) This can be a significant point of remembrance in your life.

ACTIVATION FOUR

Craft a personalized psalm heralding the Lord's faithfulness. You do not need to be a good writer to do this. I suggest you free write and write whatever comes to your mind when you think about what God has done for you in the past.

Consider what He has done and what He is doing for you now. What are you standing in faith for Him to do in your future? How does this reflect His nature and character? Write your personal psalm here.

ACTIVATION FIVE

Let's go a bit further with *our* faithfulness. Throughout this study, we have immersed ourselves in God's faithfulness to us. What about our faithfulness to God? And our faithfulness to people? And our faithfulness to what we have been given? Faithfulness is a fruit of the Spirit (Galatians 5:22-23). Daily, we take a stance for faithfulness and choose how this fruit will mature in us. We choose to be faithful to God. We choose to be faithful to others and grow in our faithfulness. Faithfulness is not a have-to—it's a want-to. Even a get-to.

> *"The one who manages the little he has been given with faithfulness and integrity will be promoted and trusted with greater responsibilities. But those who cheat with the little whey have been given will not be considered trustworthy to receive more. If you have not handled the riches of this world with integrity, why should you be trusted with the eternal treasures of the spiritual world: And if you have not been proven faithful with what belongs to another, why should you be given wealth of your own?"* (Luke 16:10-12)

How have you managed with faithfulness and integrity what you have been given? What have you been given? What gifts do you carry? How are you stewarding them? How are you faithful to God? How about others? Addressing these questions, write a list of ways you are and can be faithful.

PRAYER FOCUS: Amazing Faithfulness

God is speaking to us so clearly that He is faithful! How is your faith in God transforming from reading this chapter, posturing in the verses, and applying the activations?

HEAVENLY WORD

What does this prayer target as the core of God's character?

Video Notes

6
Trusting God
Rely on Him to Guide You

Trust doesn't always come easily. Most of us have had our trust broken. Yet over and over, the Bible reveals God is trustworthy. We can trust that He has a plan for our lives and that it is outrageously wonderful! He is a good, good Father who wants only the best for us. Trusting God means you are giving Him the wheel. It means you decided to trust Him with everything that pertains to you—your life, your future, your relationships, and your finances—everything. Whether you are just now learning to trust God or if you have trusted Him a long time, this chapter will broaden your trust walk with Him! Enter into miraculous trust!

READ PROVERBS 3:5-6, THE PASSION TRANSLATION.

Write the verse. Ponder the deeper meaning for you personally.

Based on this verse, how do we trust God? What do we do? What does He do?

What are some synonyms for trust?

READ PARAGRAPHS ONE TO THREE.

When I was diagnosed with breast cancer, I had a visceral reaction I did not anticipate: I felt shame. I was confused that this could happen to me, a Christian who loved and served God. I was ashamed and embarrassed and confused. *Is something wrong with me?* I wondered.

Has something like this happened to you? Has your faith been tested when something happened you did not understand?

Let's be real. We do not understand many of the trials we face. Yet in the Proverbs 3:5-6 passage you just wrote down, God urges us to trust Him. Do you discern what the key is? That verse ends with, *"Become intimate with Him in whatever you do, and he will lead you wherever you go."* This is huge! In the previous chapters of this study, we have deepened our intimacy with God, postured in the wind of the Spirit, and practiced entering into the secret place.

Do you see how all of these facets of your miraculous identity are fitting together? What serious challenge have you faced or are you now facing for which you chose to dig in your heels and trust God?

In your Christian walk, did you learn to trust God over time, or did it happen quickly? Explain how your trust relationship with God evolved.

READ PARAGRAPHS FOUR AND FIVE.

Trusting God means you are confident in Him—that He is _____, that He _____, and that He is _____.

If we are to grow in our ability to trust Him, it is vital for us to believe these truths in our hearts. Which ones do you most fully believe?

When we see deadlines, what does God see? _____ Trust is a decision that _____ _____.

READ PARAGRAPHS SIX TO EIGHT.

How is faith described? How do you feel about that?

Read Romans 8:28. Share a time when your life was chaotic and unsettling and you were able to hold onto the truth that God was good, and that He was *for* you.

The most meaningful season of our faith is when we continue to believe even though we are not yet seeing any fruit. When has this been true in your own life?

READ PARAGRAPHS NINE THROUGH ELEVEN.

According to Matthew 17:20, with what does Jesus associate our faith?

Now look at Matthew 13:31-32. What happens to the seed as it grows?

Share an example of how you have seen your faith grow over time.

When you _____ take steps to transform your thinking, it won't be just a head thing. It will revolutionize your _____. So, get ready for a revolution as you _____ these verses with all your heart!

POSTURING INSIGHTS: What Holds You Back from Trusting?

Speak each verse over yourself out loud. Are you getting stuck at any verses? Choose your top three "I'm stuck" verses. Write them here.

What are you telling yourself that keeps you from believing each of these verses?

Are you willing to break off your agreement with what has kept you from trusting God? Stepping into the arena of trust means breaking an agreement with anxiety and fear. But think about this: anxiety and fear are limiting. Having faith and trusting God is limitless. There is no limitation in the Spirit. To break this stronghold, pray, *"Lord, I am sorry for believing a lie. Doing so kept me from trusting You. I do trust You. In Jesus' Name, I break my agreement with that lie. I command the bondage broken! From now on, I believe. ..."* Say the verse again in your own words. Write what is new and real and true for you here.

EXPERIENTIAL ACTIVATIONS: You can Trust God with Your Life

ACTIVATION ONE

When circumstances in our lives challenge our faith and trust in God, we must be ready to fight the good fight of faith. We do this with the Word of God. Declare these posturing verses out loud twice a day, morning and night, for a week. Release them over the circumstances of your life. See yourself becoming an intentional speaker, saturating yourself with truths. Declaring that which is true transforms you inside. Also, choose ten verses and continue to declare them for the next thirty days. The fruit of your inner work will manifest in your daily life. Becoming aligned with how God sees you changes your life. Your faith and trust is ever increasing.

How has posturing changed you over the last few weeks?

One-Week Verse Recitations Check-Off List (all 49)

Day	Sunday	Monday	Tuesday	Wednesday	Thursday	Friday	Saturday
Morning							
Bedtime							

Thirty-Day Verse Recitations Check-Off List (10 favorites)

Verse / day	1	2	3	4	5	6	7	8	9	10
1										
2										
3										
4										
5										
6										
7										
8										
9										
10										
11										
12										
13										
14										
15										
16										
17										
18										
19										
20										
21										
22										
23										
24										

25									
26									
27									
28									
29									
30									

Describe the reaction of your inner spirit to these verse recitations.

ACTIVATION TWO

Through the generations, the Israelites passed on the history of God's intervention in their lives. They told stories of these mighty miracles to their children and to their children's children. Events were commemorated by naming locations, people, and cities after the miracles and encounters with God. They made sure they remembered what God had done for them.

Ask the Holy Spirit to show you specific times in the past when you trusted God. Close your eyes and relive what God did for you. Write your story of God's intervention in your life. Just like the Israelites, you can pass on stories of the miracles God has done for you.

ACTIVATION THREE

Go with a friend on a "trust walk" in your neighborhood. This activation may challenge you, which is why I suggest you do this with someone you really trust. Hold your friend's hand, close your eyes, and let him or her lead you on a walk. With your eyes closed, touch flowers, trees, buildings. You can even try walking fast. Consider how it feels to no longer be in control. This exercise would be a starting place in the natural realm.

The God of all creation has wonderous places to show you and revelations to give you. Your life with God is a trust walk. The spiritual senses of your miraculous identity are developing. He will walk with you, run with you, have you touch and see and smell in the miraculous.

If you were able to go on a trust walk with a friend, how did you feel on the walk? Was it easy, difficult, scary, fun? (If you're in a Bible Study, you can take time right now to do the "trust walk" with your group.)

Imagine how can you apply this experience to your walk with God. Experiment. Close your eyes and go on an inner trust walk with God. What would that be like? Do you think He might like to show you heavenly treasures?

ACTIVATION FOUR

Read Philippians 1:6 in a few translations. God began a good work in you and will continue developing that good work. What specific areas in your character are you trusting God to bring to full completion in you? What specific ways are you doing what you need to do to cooperate with God's work in you?

What dreams and visions do you want to see God fulfill in your lifetime? It's okay to dream big! Quickly, jot them down. Don't over-think this or you will likely put limits on your dreams. Remove the limitations.

Again, how are you doing your part? Many Christians think all they need do is sit back, wait, and do nothing. But this is a relationship. He loves for us to work together with Him. Remember: Faith without works is dead.

PRAYER FOCUS: MIRACULOUS TRUST

Pray the prayer in the book and anoint yourself with oil as you read the prayer. Using olive oil (or whatever you have on hand), anoint yourself as a symbolic way of consecrating yourself as one who trusts God daily.

HEAVENLY WORD

Read the Heavenly Word in the book. What a loving, intimate word! What does this reveal about God's character?

Video Notes

Video Notes

7
Miraculous Peace
Fear and Anxiety Cannot Have You

Jericho could well be called the City of Anxiety. Enormous walls surrounded the large, intimidating city. How could the Israelites possess it? How could they penetrate it? What the Lord directed them to do did not seem reasonable: Walk around it seven times and then holler for all you're worth? But it worked. God was right in the middle of the fight, and the people followed His lead. Jesus already gave us peace. It is in you right now. To possess the manifestation of peace in your life, follow His lead, and the peace of God will guard your heart and your mind.

WRITE ISAIAH 26:3 FROM THE AMPLIFIED BIBLE

What is our part? What do we do to live in perfect and constant peace?

Look up Proverbs 3:5-6. What does this passage tell us about trusting, leaning, and acknowledging?

READ PARAGRAPHS ONE AND TWO

"I had to take hold of my one and only lifeline. I had to. I must align my thoughts with heaven. I had to see myself through God's eyes. Riding on a wave of His word was my only hope. My mind had to be steadfast, trusting in Him, believing in Him, relying on Him."

When have you had to take hold of your one-and-only lifeline? What did you do?

"Over the ensuing weeks, my voice grew stronger. *"I have hope and I have a future."* In the middle of the night, when loneliness was pressing down on me, I said this over and over. During the day, those words kept me moving forward. The Holy Spirit was strengthening me as I agreed with heaven about my future. I am not saying it was easy."

What did you say to yourself? Were you able to agree with heaven? For me, it was not easy. I had to persevere. How about you?

"Peace about my having a future without my husband dropped from my mind down into my spirit. Excitement came. Joy came. Enthusiasm came. I started working on my next book."

As you have been speaking the posturing verses and rewiring your mindsets to agree with heaven, transformation has been occurring inside. In what ways have verses dropped down from your mind into your spirit? Explain.

READ PARAGRAPHS THREE TO FIVE

"If Jesus came to give me peace, why does it seem so hard to receive sometimes?"

Answer this question.

What does it mean to fight *from* victory, not *toward* victory?

"Second, we have an antagonist, a thief that comes to _____, _____, _____ _____ our peace. His main tactic: _____. The battle over fear is _____."

What are the main battles you fight in the war between your ears?

READ PARAGRAPHS SIX THROUGH EIGHT

"The robber of peace is fear. Fear _____ us. Fear paralyzes us and gets us to make _____ if not inferior decisions. It robs us of the joy and breakthrough that comes from being courageous and _____. It keeps our dreams at bay.

MIRACULOUS PEACE

Many of us have goals and dreams. Does fear hold you back from achieving those goals and dreams? What would you do if fear was not an issue?

"Anxiety brings peace-stealing thoughts like these: *Your future looks bleak. You're going to fail. You're not going to survive this. You'll never get this bill paid off.* And those thoughts can assault every one of us."

What distressing thoughts come to you to steal your peace?

READ PARAGRAPPHS NINE THROUGH ELEVEN

Many of us feel there are not enough hours in the day. Perhaps, you don't get your daily "to do" list done. How is not having enough time stressful for you?

"_____ does not concern God. He stands outside time. He has made the way for you to _____ every obstacle and find a _____ as you do it. Here is the BIG KEY: *God gives you enough _____ to do everything He has called you to do.*"

READ PARAGRAPHS TWELVE THROUGH FOURTEEN

What passages in Psalm 23 really minister to you?

What thoughts and images come to mind when you consider God preparing a table for you in the presence of your enemies?

POSTURING INSIGHTS: Read through the Posturing Declarations Out Loud with the Next Question in Mind.

Which verse registers with you as the most powerful?

List three verses you have a hard time saying and believing?

What mindset hinders you from believing these verses?

If the verse is true, the mindset is not. That mindset is a lie. Get this. 2 Corinthians 11:3 reads:

"But I am afraid that just as Eve was deceived by the serpent's cunning, your minds may somehow be led astray from your sincere and pure devotion to Christ."

Our *minds* can be deceived. Ask Holy Spirit to show you the deception. What lie is trying to stand in the place of truth? Once you see the lie, break your agreement with it, and say, *"Wow, God, I just didn't realize I was believing a deception. Forgive me. I'm tearing down that lie. I believe You and what You say!"* Write about this here.

Fear and anxiety do not exist in heaven. They do not come from God. God has not given you a spirit of fear. You can command fear and anxiety to leave you. You can say, *"God has not given me the spirit of fear but of power and of love and of a sound mind. Fear, leave me now in Jesus' name. Anxiety, I command you to go, in Jesus' name. Amen."* Now, pick up the book and declare the Posturing Declarations: Peace is Yours.

EXPERIENTIAL ACTIVATIONS: Peace is Yours

ACTIVATION ONE

Proclaim the Peace is Yours verses twice a day for seven days. You are establishing a daily routine. Begin your day saying the personalized verses and again at night before bed. After one week, choose ten verses to include in your thirty-day posturing list. Track your days below.

One-Week Verse Recitations Check-Off List (all 36)

Day	Sunday	Monday	Tuesday	Wednesday	Thursday	Friday	Saturday
Morning							
Bedtime							

Thirty-Day Verse Recitations Check-Off List (10 favorites)

<u>Verse</u> day	1	2	3	4	5	6	7	8	9	10
1										
2										
3										

4										
5										
6										
7										
8										
9										
10										
11										
12										
13										
14										
15										
16										
17										
18										
19										
20										
21										
22										
23										
24										
25										
26										
27										
28										
29										
30										

Describe the reaction of your inner spirit to these verse recitations.

ACTIVATION TWO

What is stealing your peace? Make a list of things in your life that cause you fear, stress, or anxiety. What are your top three points of concern? Write your list.

Read over your list and ask yourself, *"Do I want to keep these worries and fears?"* Draw a line through the ones you do not want to keep.

As you can see from my story at the beginning of the chapter, you do not have to remain subject to your inner turmoil. Your starting place is to simply give your list to God. Cast it all on Him. The Passion Translation of 1 Peter 5:7 reads as follows:

"Pour out all your worries and stress upon him and leave them there, for he always tenderly cares for you."

In other words, give it all over to Him. Why? Because He cares for you. The Lord tells us not to be anxious. He is literally saying that we are to transfer the burden of our soul over to Him. This is huge. Do not take it lightly! Seriously, *transfer all your burdens to Him!* At the bottom of your list, write: *"I give all this to You, Lord."*

He then tells us to be thankful and pray. At that point, He will help us. God Himself will put a *guard* around our minds and hearts so we can have peace. This is the answer you have been looking for. Guarding your heart and mind is not a small matter! *"…the idea is not merely that of protection, but of inward garrisoning as by the Holy Spirit"* (Vines, p. 284).

A garrison of peace is also a big deal! It is a body of troops stationed in a fortified place. Talk about protection. God is saying if you give your anxiety over to Him, then He will put troops around your mind. And your heart! His guard is an inward protection. Philippians 4:6-7 describes the whole enchilada:

> *"Do not be anxious about anything, but in everything, by prayer and petition, with thanksgiving, present your requests to God. And the peace of God, which transcends all understanding, will guard your hearts and your minds in Christ Jesus."*

Many places in the Bible instruct us not to worry. Take your anxiety list into the secret place and give it to God. Burn it, wad it up, throw it in the trash—whatever it takes. Give Him your list. Thank Him for the inner guard around your heart and mind that keeps peace within you. Take a couple deep breaths and read back over the posturing verses.

ACTIVATION THREE

Most of us have certain people who always tend to bring chaos and drama into our lives. Evaluate how much access God wants you to give them into your life. Is God really calling you to them? If so, what boundaries do you need to enforce? Keep in mind, true peace does not involve making treaties at the expense of giving away pieces of your life. Be real. Be honest. Ask God for help. Write your thoughts about this activation.

ACTIVATION FOUR

A trigger point for worry often springs from trying to juggle an overloaded schedule. We must pace ourselves as we run the race. Yes, we can all have extra-busy seasons—but that can't be the norm or you will burn out. It's when we are overly tired that fear and anxiety taunt us. Setting some schedule boundaries is a good first step to recapturing peace. Remember, you have enough time to do everything God has called you to do. If you are overloaded and worn out, look at what's on your plate. Take your big plate to the Throne Room and ask God what stays and what goes.

PRAYER FOCUS: PEACE

In the book, Read Prayer Focus: Peace. What would you want to add to the prayer?

HEAVENLY WORD

This word is so beautiful! Jehovah Shalom, the Source of all peace! Jesus is peace, and He lives in you. Beloved, peace already resides in you. The verse references below the Heavenly Word are rich. Don't rush. Take your time. Read and savor each verse.

Video Notes

8
Wondrous Realms of Knowing and Experiencing God
Personal, Intimate, and Real

The most valuable relationship we have in life is *knowing* God. The most astounding encounters we can have in life would be *experiencing* God. If we can recite all the verses about His love but do not *experience* His love, we will continue to be stuck battling strongholds in our lives. All our decisions, thoughts, and actions flow from how we experience Him. Getting to know Him is a process that takes time. Reading His love letter to us, tells us about His nature and character. Every day we can grow closer to Him. Every day we can see Him working in our lives. Every day new facets of His love and faithfulness are revealed. How do you see God? As Father? As Friend? As the lover of your soul? How do you experience Him as the One who knows everything about you and loves you most?

READ JEREMIAH 9:24 IN A FEW DIFFERENT TRANSLATIONS.

Why do you think it is more important for us to boast in the Lord and not in our wisdom or strength?

What three qualities about God do we experience from knowing Him?

Why is it important for us to know that God *delights* in these qualities?

READ THE FIRST TWO PARAGRAPHS AND ANSWER THE FOLLOWING QUESTIONS.

What would you tell someone who says, "I don't know how to know God"?

What are some ways you have gotten to know God over the years? Through His Word? By praying? Other ways?

Before reading this chapter, what did you know about God's character?

What two ways does God primarily reveal Himself to us?

READ PARAGRAPHS THREE TO FIVE.

List all the attributes of God mentioned in paragraph three.

As we get to know God, we can recognize ways He engages with us. What does "engage" mean?

Which of these characteristics of God do you need most in your life right now? Explain why.

What facets of God are indicated in paragraphs four and five?

READ PARAGRAPHS SIX THROUGH THIRTEEN.

"The heart of this chapter is not only to *know* God, but most importantly to *experience* God." To know God is so personal and intimate that this Greek word is also used to describe physical intimacy between a man and a woman. Write John 17:3 from the Passion Translation.

You can know of God and about God, but it is in your spiritual DNA to _____ _____ God. To know Him is to have _____ _____ knowledge of the highest level. You are _____, and God encounters you in ways that are _____ _____ to you.

What are some practical ways to *pursue God* and recognize Him?

LOOK AT THE LAST TWO PARAGRAPHS AND ANSWER THE FOLLOWING QUESTIONS.

What is a primary block that keeps us from recognizing Him?

Why does this keep us from recognizing Him?

Knowing by experience what He is like enables us to _____ and _____ from heavenly places.

According to the last paragraph, we are to be militant and worshipful in our declarations. Why?

POSTURING INSIGHTS: READ THROUGH THE POSTURING DECLARATIONS OUT LOUD WITH THE NEXT QUESTIONS IN MIND.

Share three verses that you absolutely love.

How do you feel inside when you declare these verses?

We "demolish arguments and every pretension that sets itself up against the *knowledge of God*" (2 Corinthians 10:5). Choose a verse you had a hard time fully believing and write it down.

Ask God to show you why you had a difficult time believing the verse. What if there is a lie blocking your ability to see the truth. What is the lie? Is there more than one?

Quiet your heart and ask God to forgive you for believing the lie. Verbally break the agreement you have had with the lie. Say, *"Lord, I am sorry for believing the lie. It kept me from believing Your Word. In Jesus' Name, I break my agreement with that lie. The bondage is broken. From now on, I believe..."* (Say the verse again in your own words.)

Invite God into that place in your heart that perhaps was wounded. Let Him bring restoration to the places in your heart that need to know more of Him. Say, *"Lord, heal the injured place in my heart when the lie came in. Restore me."* Share your thoughts.

EXPERIENTIAL ACTIVATIONS: KNOWING AND EXPERIENCING GOD MORE FULLY

ACTIVATION ONE

Say the Posturing Declarations twice a day, morning and night. Choose ten verses to continue speaking for thirty days. You can track your time on the charts below. As a result of your on-going posturing, what kind of changes are you seeing in yourself or how you experience God?

One-Week Verse Recitations Check-Off List (all 28)

Day	Sunday	Monday	Tuesday	Wednesday	Thursday	Friday	Saturday
Morning							
Bedtime							

Thirty-Day Verse Recitations Check-Off List (10 favorites)

Verse / day	1	2	3	4	5	6	7	8	9	10
1										
2										
3										
4										
5										
6										
7										

8										
9										
10										
11										
12										
13										
14										
15										
16										
17										
18										
19										
20										
21										
22										
23										
24										
25										
26										
27										
28										
29										
30										

Describe the reaction of your inner spirit to these verse recitations.

ACTIVATION TWO

We are becoming more in tune to how God is engaging with us. Engage means to occupy the attention or efforts of a person. Ask Holy Spirit to show you how God has engaged with you in the past twenty-four hours. When have you sensed God engaging with you? In can be in conversations, while driving, shopping, watching a movie (He talks to me often when I go see a film!), during prayer, listening to music, or any type of situation. Write about His presence in your life and ways he is engaging with you.

ACTIVATION THREE

Read about God's characteristics in the following paragraphs from chapter eight.

"We know that He's the God of all Comfort, that He's our Peace, and our Healer, healing our hearts as well as our bodies. He is also our Provider, our Shepherd, Restorer, Refuge, Judge, Hope, Righteousness, and our beloved, personal, and very good Papa. He is a consuming fire, destroying everything opposed to His holiness. He is holy—completely. He is personally involved with you to the degree that you will let Him. Everything about you holds His attention. As you get to know Him, He engages with you. To engage means to attract and hold fast, to occupy the attention of, to become involved with and secure for aid.

He gives you grace to accomplish all He calls you to do. His grace and mercy endure forever. He is jealous for you and loves to spend time with you. He loves to guide you and reveal new things to you. He leads you into places of rest and places of war. He enables you to succeed at both. His banner over you is love. With Him, you can overcome any enemy. He is God Almighty—nothing is impossible for Him.

He is love, and He pours out His love on you day and night, with kisses from heaven. He is the One who sees you and knows everything about you. He is the Most High—nothing, no one, is higher. He has all power, all authority, and all sovereignty. He is the Ruler of all things. He is the Alpha and Omega, the beginning and the end. He shows up in your life all day long—and throughout the night. He is the stay-up-late-and-talk-about-everything friend. Look for Him and engage with Him."

During major trauma and huge triumphs in your life, which of these characteristics of God have you experienced?

ACTIVATION FOUR

To have a profound activation requires a set-apart time for a heart-to-heart communion with God. Psalm 42:2 reads, *"My soul thirsts for God, for the living God. When can I go and meet with God?"* Now is your time. Meet with your Creator. The One who knows everything about you and loves you. He is knocking on the door. Open the door and go in.

Read the attributes of God to help prepare your heart. Take the posturing verses with you as you enter into the secret place. Be real. Be yourself.

PRAYER: Pursuing God

Pray Psalm 63:1 (Passion Translation) as though these are your own words. Add a few lines of your own to this prayer.

HEAVENLY WORD

Read the Heavenly Word and look up the reference verses written below it.

Video Notes

Video Notes

9
Getting Pictures from God
Dreaming with God

You live in two worlds: One is the natural realm, which is this physical world. The other is God's realm, which is a world of the miraculous. You could say these realms overlap. While you see with your physical eyes what is before you in the physical world, you can also "see" into God's world. It is God who opens your eyes and gives you access into His unseen realm. It can be brief glimpses of images, clear pictures as Peter with the unclean animals, vivid dreams or scattered pieces of dreams. Because images often do not make sense to us, these pictures require us to engage with God and find out what to do with the revelation God gives us. Some people, like Elisha's servant (2 Kings 6:15-17), see a living-color video played out before their eyes. Many times, pictures are for you personally—to encourage you, strengthen you, and bring you comfort. As you are being transformed through the renewing of your mind, the place in you where images reside is developing. Just relax. Breathe. Don't force anything. God will show you what He wants you to see.

READ JEREMIAH 33:3 AMP IN THE BOOK.

What are the absolute facts stated in this verse?

How does this truth affect you?

READ PARAGRAPHS ONE AND TWO.

Think of a picture God has given you. How has it continued to minister to you over time?

LOOK AT PARAGRAPHS THREE, FOUR, AND FIVE.

One of the ways God speaks to us is by giving us _____. Sometimes we also receive _____ revelation. Sometimes revelation comes _____ _____. Sometimes the image is only a _____ _____ _____ while at other times the picture can be a more _____ _____.

God shows us _____ of which we have no knowledge. Whether He speaks in a whisper or with a quick glimpse of a picture, He is teaching us to _____ to His leading.

Renewing your mind includes renewing _____ as well.

Your mind is a great _____. Satan wants to _____ it. The war is not only for your thoughts, but also for the _____ in your mind. The place in your mind where images are planted belongs to _____. The Bible teaches us to pull down _____ _____. Your mind is to be filled with _____ and _____.

In paragraph five, you see that renewing your mind includes not only thoughts but also images. Just as you don't have to allow thoughts to remain, you can also pull down images. You can have pre-arranged "go to" images. Ask the Holy Spirit what images you can think of when an ungodly image tries to take hold of your mind. Just as you are ready with verses when a mental attack comes, be ready with godly images. Write down three godly "go to" images.

LOOK AT PARAGRAPHS SIX AND SEVEN AND ANSWER THE FOLLOWING.

Describe an image you saw when you were praying for someone.

The purpose of pictures is to receive _____ into matters that are on God's heart. Pictures _____ you, give you _____, and _____ in the right direction. Getting a picture from God helps us become aware of God's purposes and helps us cooperate with Him. Think of a time when you engaged more with God because you received a picture from Him.

The Holy Spirit is the ultimate _____, and He reveals things to us through _____ and _____. The _____ of the Holy Spirit often manifest in us also by way of thoughts and images. Revelation through images _____ the gifts of the Spirit.

What are some examples of how images can be involved in the gifts of the Holy Spirit? (Word of knowledge, word of wisdom, healing, prophecy, discerning of spirits, faith, miracles, speaking in tongues and the interpretation of tongues (1 Corinthians 12:7-11).

READ PARAGRPHS EIGHT TO ELEVEN

In these paragraphs, what about these Bible passages impacted you most?

Share a significant dream you've had that you strongly felt came from God.

READ PARAGRAPHS TWELVE THROUGH FIFTEEN.

What does it mean for you to consecrate your mind?

Pray the prayer for consecrating your mind. After you pray, close your eyes and ask Holy Spirit what else He would add to this prayer for you. What does He tell you?

What about the entire teaching section impacted you the most?

POSTURING INSIGHTS: Read through the Posturing Declarations Out Loud with the Next Questions in Mind.

Which declarations are your favorites?

What top three declarations do you have trouble believing?

Ask God to show you why you had a difficult time believing the verses. What if there is a lie blocking your ability to see the truth. What would the lie be? Is there more than one?

Quiet your heart and ask God to forgive you for believing the lie. Verbally break the agreement you have had with the lie. Say *"Lord, I am sorry for believing the lie. It kept me from believing Your Word. In Jesus' Name, I break my agreement with that lie. The bondage is broken. From now on, I believe. ..."* (Say the verse again in your own words.)

Invite God into that place in your heart that perhaps was wounded. Let Him bring restoration to the places in your heart that need to know more of Him. Say, *"Lord, heal the injured place in my heart when the lie came in. Restore me."* Share your thoughts.

EXPERIENTIAL ACTIVATIONS: Opening Up Your Spiritual Senses

ACTIVATION ONE

Posturing in Getting Pictures from God is high-level posturing because you are endeavoring to purposefully activate your spiritual senses. You are making yourself available to the Holy Spirit and adamantly saying, "I receive! I receive all You want to show me!"

Speak these verses twice a day—morning and night. Vain imaginations must go. You are taking some serious ground. Right now, say, "Lord, in Jesus' name, the place in me where images live belongs to You!"

Choose ten verses to continue to say for the next thirty days. To track your progress, you can use these charts. The charts are intended to be a support to you—not for you to use to beat yourself up should you not wish to use them.

One-Week Verse Recitations Check-Off List (all 22)

Day	Sunday	Monday	Tuesday	Wednesday	Thursday	Friday	Saturday
Morning							
Bedtime							

Thirty-Day Verse Recitations Check-Off List (10 favorites)

Verse day	1	2	3	4	5	6	7	8	9	10
1										
2										
3										
4										
5										
6										
7										
8										

9										
10										
11										
12										
13										
14										
15										
16										
17										
18										
19										
20										
21										
22										
23										
24										
25										
26										
27										
28										
29										
30										

Describe the reaction of your inner spirit to these verse recitations.

ACTIVATION TWO

Read 2 Kings 6:8-14. God supernaturally allowed Elisha to know what the king of Aram was speaking in the privacy of his bedroom. Elisha *heard* what was being spoken. Maybe he even *saw* what went on in the king's quarters. We do not know how many of Elisha's spiritual senses were discerning the spirit realm in this event.

Keep reading through verses 15–17. Elijah could see into the spirit realm. God revealed that the hills were full of horses and chariots of fire. We know Elisha was not afraid, because he told his servant not to be afraid. When your spiritual eyes are opened and you see from God's perspective, you will experience changes inside. Fear goes. Anxiety goes. Limiting mindsets go.

Elisha prayed for his servant's eyes to be opened to the realm of the Spirit, and his eyes were opened. Now it's your turn. Ask the Lord to open your eyes. Just ask. Like you asked God to save you and fill you with the Holy Spirit. The how, when, what, why, and where is up to God. It may be now and it may be later. What you are doing is saying "YES!" to God for your eyes to be opened.

Pray: *Father, just as Elisha prayed for his servant's eyes to be opened, I ask You to open my eyes that I might see in the realm of the Spirit. I want to see what You are doing and see things from Your perspective so I can come to a place of higher revelation. You said for me to fix my eyes on what is unseen. I do so now. I yield my eyes to You now. Open my spiritual eyes to the realm of the unseen. According to Your purposes and Your plans for me, I ask for all you have for me—including more visions, more dreams, more revelations, and more supernatural encounters with You. In the Name of the Lord Jesus Christ, I pray. Amen.*

Are you feeling excited? Expectant? Full of wonder? Write your thoughts.

ACTIVATION THREE

Practice "seeing with God." During your prayer times, ask Him to give you insight about something that has been on your heart. As you sit quietly in His presence, wait and watch. If He impresses you with a picture, write it down here.

Ask the Lord to reveal what the picture means. He may tell you right away, or He may want you to press in to Him for more understanding. Sometimes I just "know" what the picture means. Other times, my understanding of the picture unfolds over time. Go to the Bible and look up references that talk about the picture. Watch for confirmations. A confirmation can be found in anything: a billboard, a song, a sunset, a movie (Yes! He has spoken to me in movies so much that I took notes in the dark!) or in what seems to be an idle conversation. Watch. What do you sense thus far?

ACTIVATION FOUR

Your spiritual sight is only one of your spiritual senses. Activate all your spiritual senses to not only see, but also to hear, feel, smell, and taste. Hebrews 5:14, Passion Translation, says, *"But solid food is for the mature, whose spiritual senses perceive heavenly matters."*

I teach a lot from Romans 12:2, but this verse is preceded by Romans 12:1—a crucial verse about presenting our entire selves as a living sacrifice to God. Amplified says, *"…to make a decisive dedication of your bodies [presenting all your members and faculties] as a living sacrifice, holy (devoted, consecrated) and well pleasing to God, which is your reasonable (rational, intelligent) service and spiritual worship."* I take it to mean *all* your senses.

Pray: *Father, I activate all my spiritual senses. I want to be fully engaged with you! Activate all my spiritual senses to not only see, but also to hear, feel, smell, and taste. I offer my whole self as a living sacrifice, holy and pleasing to You—which is my spiritual worship. Transform me! Amen.*

Write your thoughts on this activation.

ACTIVATION FIVE

Read 1 Corinthians 2:10-16 and John 16:13-15 in a few translations. The Holy Spirit guides us, speaks to us, and reveals things to us. To *reveal* means to make known something that was previously secret or unknown. It is to bring a hidden thing to the open. The Holy Spirit makes things known that are unknown or hidden, and in doing so He helps us navigate through challenging waters. He is a revealer of divine secrets. Think of a specific situation you need God to guide you through. Using these verses, talk to Him about your situation. Ask Him to reveal hidden things about this situation.

Write what God shows you.

PRAYER FOCUS: Seeing from Heavenly Realms

You have been soaking in truths and concepts about receiving from heaven. You are seated in heavenly realms with Christ Jesus. What does it mean to see from this heavenly realm position?

HEAVENLY WORD

I can feel the Holy Spirit stirring within so deeply. I sense that even now, He is responding to your hunger and pouring out more and more into you. Gently and quietly, speak this Heavenly Word over yourself. Then just sit still and let it saturate your being. When you are ready, write a prayer back to God.

Video Notes

10
Encourage Yourself in the Lord
Your Hidden Journey Dramatically Shifts

Encouraging yourself in the Lord is not a motivational pep talk—it is a miraculous transport into an otherworldly dimension of power, strength, and endurance. Decreeing words of life and truth over yourself is to agree with God Himself. When you have nothing to help you, no one to hold you, what do you do to encourage yourself? When you dig down deep, what uplifting words are deep in your spirit? What will you say to yourself when all is lost? When, on this last leg of your hidden journey, the core of your very being—the real you—goes through the fire, what will remain?

READ THE ABOVE PARAGRAPH AND ANSWER THE QUESTIONS IN THE PARAGRAPH.

WRITE 1 SAMUEL 30:6 FROM THE AMPLIFIED BIBLE.

Sometimes, we go through such difficulties that we feel like we can barely breathe. Can you relate? "Greatly distressed" means to bind up, tie up, be restricted. Share about a time when you were greatly distressed and felt bound up.

In the middle of the verse, we find a big "but." In other words, in spite of everything said before the big "but," something happened next that altered everything. What happened? Why do you think this was possible?

Rather than describing God as the "God of Israel" or the "God of Abraham, Isaac, and Jacob," The passage states that "David strengthened and encouraged himself in the LORD *his* God." God is not referred to as a historical God but a personal, ever-present God in the "now" of David's life. The real God. The true. The miraculous. I believe it is because David experienced God so intimately and personally that he could not describe God as anything but "his" God.

As you have been posturing in this course and drawing close to God, has the way you would describe God changed? Expanded? Do you see Him as "your" God?

READ PARAGRAPHS ONE THROUGH FOUR

In the past, how have you been able to overcome discouragement? What was the situation?

The root of the word "encourage" is "to fasten upon." How do you think David fastened himself upon the Lord?

What are some of the miracles you could encourage yourself with?

What truths about God encourage you?

READ PARAGRAPHS FIVE TO TEN

In paragraph eight, you see you have two choices before you when you are in a difficult season: You can give up or you can get strong. This doesn't mean you don't feel the pain, the hurt, and the anguish. We are created with emotions. We feel. And it is important to feel. But it is a slippery slope if we set up camp there. God is with you in every kind of season. It is your choice to look up and allow encouragement from heaven to flow into your life. It is your choice to watch for Jesus' footsteps, and your choice to follow Him.

"We rarely think about encouraging _____. Today, all this is going to _____. You are going to stand in the path of God's _____ and feel His words of encouragement _____ _____ _____."

According to 1 Corinthians 14:3, when we speak prophetically to someone, what are we doing?

ENCOURAGE YOURSELF IN THE LORD

Give some examples of encouraging prophetic words that have been spoken over your life.

> **POSTURING INSIGHTS:** READ THROUGH THE POSTURING DECLARATIONS OUT LOUD WITH THE NEXT QUESTIONS IN MIND.

Choose three verses that are hard for you to speak or believe. Write them here.

It can be almost unthinkable to consider encouraging ourselves. Even when we look fine on the outside, we can beat ourselves up on the inside. I know leaders and pastors who admit they are hard on themselves. A common belief is that we are not doing enough and that we do not measure up. Here is the truth: You *do* measure up—now listen to me—because of the blood of Jesus. You are righteous because of *Him*. Take your hands off yourself. God doesn't want anyone treating you cruelly—even *yourself*. Honor His creation—*you!* Love His creation—*you!*

Look at the verses that are hard to align yourself with and ask Holy Spirit, *"What am a really believing instead of these encouraging words?"* Ask Him to reveal the lie. Write the lie below.

You can talk this over with the Lord with the following prayer, but by now you know this step. Either follow this prayer or use your own words. You are doing great. I wish I could see you at this stage of the study. *"God, I am sorry for my lack of trust and how so many times I am harsh with myself. If anything, I do not want to discourage myself. I choose to speak life and purposefully encourage myself. I am so sorry. Right now, I align myself with how You see me. In Jesus' name, Amen."*

EXPERIENTIAL ACTIVATIONS: Encouraging Yourself

ACTIVATION ONE

To transform the way we talk to ourselves, we have to replace words of self-limitation and discouragement with biblical words of encouragement. This means we purposefully take *action*. That's the beauty of this activation. You now have a solid tool in your hand to strengthen yourself and find ongoing encouragement. Speak the posturing verses to yourself twice a day. Begin in front of the mirror. Pointing to yourself at times for emphasis. Then, after a few days, pace and speak over yourself. For one week. Do this first thing when you get up and last thing before bed.

Choose ten verses to continue speaking for the next thirty days. By the end of this course, you will have 100 verses. It sounds like a lot, but it will take you about twenty minutes. Don't stress. The Lord told Joshua to think about and speak the word day and night. You can do this. The more you do, the stronger you become. Often, I take the verses on my morning walk and then I will keep them in the car so they are easily accessible to me throughout the day.

After thirty days, you can change out the verses. Yes, posturing (renewing your mind) is a lifelong affair. Remember, renewing your mind *transforms* you. But *you* are the one who does the act of renewing. It is for *you* to do.

Again, this chart is provided as a support tool, not to use to beat yourself up. Posturing twice a day is not meant to be a legalistic approach, but rather to establish a foundation for proactively renewing your mind.

One-Week Verse Recitations Check-Off List (all 45)

Day	Sunday	Monday	Tuesday	Wednesday	Thursday	Friday	Saturday
Morning							
Bedtime							

Thirty-Day Verse Recitations Check-Off List (10 favorites)

Verse / day	1	2	3	4	5	6	7	8	9	10
1										
2										
3										

4										
5										
6										
7										
8										
9										
10										
11										
12										
13										
14										
15										
16										
17										
18										
19										
20										
21										
22										
23										
24										
25										
26										
27										
28										
29										
30										

Describe the reaction of your inner spirit to these verse recitations.

ACTIVATION TWO

Ask Holy Spirit a very important question: *"Holy Spirit, what words do I need to say to myself? What do I need to hear?"* When I have taught identity intensives, I have directed people to ask Holy Spirit this question. Over and over again, I see each person know what he/she needs to hear. It will be something positive and encouraging that perhaps you have a hard time saying to yourself. It could be something like, *"You're beautiful. You're lovable. You're smart. Life is worth living. You have heavenly gifts within you to share with the world."* Look deep into your eyes in the mirror and say this Holy-Spirit-inspired truth.

How did Holy Spirit direct you? What words did you need to tell yourself? How did it feel?

ACTIVATION THREE

What is a challenging situation you are currently dealing with in your life? Ask Holy Spirit what you could say to yourself that would be encouraging.

Ask Him what verse reflects this. Write the verse and say it to yourself right now.

What is going on deep inside? Is there another verse? Get out your Bible and look up verses that deal with what you are going through. What do you learn from them?

ACTIVATION FOUR

How do you make yourself strong? Yes! By aligning yourself with every Word that proceeds from the mouth of God. Read Luke 4:1-14. How did Jesus face temptation? Having verses to stand on is exactly what Jesus did when Satan tempted Him in the wilderness. Jesus replied with, *"It is written!"* Do you think we could view this as how Jesus encouraged Himself and made Himself strong? What are your thoughts?

PRAYER FOCUS: ENCOURAGING MYSELF

Read through the prayer in the book. What impacts you the most? What would you add to the prayer?

HEAVENLY WORD

Read the Heavenly Word, letting every part of it wash over you. How has this focus on encouraging yourself affected you? Look up the references below the Heavenly Word.

Video Notes

About Linda

Linda Breitman Ministries, located in San Diego, California, is a nationally recognized force behind women's groups, faith-based ministries, and church-based Bible Studies. She has been a featured speaker for AGlow Conferences, International Women's ministries, Jubilee Conferences and a featured guest on Christian Broadcast News, Igniting a Nation, Money Talk with Melanie, The Hard Question with Blanquita Cullum and many more radio and TV programs.

She is the author of The Real You Identity Courses and has spearheaded the Prophetic Intercession Training Schools and Dangerous Women Activation Seminars.

She hosts a weekly podcast which features authors, leaders, and speakers in the church community; leaders defeating child abuse, sexual assault, ending teen homelessness; providing job opportunities for military spouses, and tackling the many social issues that canvas our society. To hear Linda's latest podcast please visit: www.lindabreitman.com

For More Information about Linda Breitman, visit:

www.lindabreitman.com

Let's Connect....

- Facebook: www.facebook.com/LindaBreitman
- Twitter: www.twitter.com/LindaBreitman
- Instagram: www.instagram.com/LindaBreitman
- YouTube: www.youtube.com/LindaBreitman

Resources

MIRACULOUS IDENTITY:

Unveiling Your Hidden Journey Curriculum

Featuring Teaching Components

- Miraculous Identity: Unveiling Your Hidden Journey
- Miraculous Identity: Study Guide
- Miraculous Identity: Video Series
- Miraculous Identity: Coaching Series
- The Real You: Believing Your True Identity
- The Real You: Activation Manual
- The Real You Video Series
- The Real You Identity Decrees
- The Real You Identity Decrees CD
- The Real You Video Sessions for Leaders
- Soaking In Your True Identity CD

These items can be purchased at:

www.LindaBreitman.com

www.ingramcontent.com/pod-product-compliance
Lightning Source LLC
Chambersburg PA
CBHW081328190426
43193CB00044B/2892